And so we did it: An experience of systematization of the DHPV course

Maritza Puertas de Rodriguez

And so we did it: An experience of systematization of the DHIPV course

ScienciaScripts

Imprint

Any brand names and product names mentioned in this book are subject to trademark, brand or patent protection and are trademarks or registered trademarks of their respective holders. The use of brand names, product names, common names, trade names, product descriptions etc. even without a particular marking in this work is in no way to be construed to mean that such names may be regarded as unrestricted in respect of trademark and brand protection legislation and could thus be used by anyone.

Cover image: www.ingimage.com

This book is a translation from the original published under ISBN 978-620-0-03408-3.

Publisher:
Sciencia Scripts
is a trademark of
Dodo Books Indian Ocean Ltd. and OmniScriptum S.R.L publishing group

120 High Road, East Finchley, London, N2 9ED, United Kingdom
Str. Armeneasca 28/1, office 1, Chisinau MD-2012, Republic of Moldova, Europe

ISBN: 978-620-7-00826-1

Table of Contents :

For man, the important thing is not what nature has given him, but what he gives himself, not to manage his assets, but to choose his being.

Albert Jacquard

SUMMARY

The adventure and the challenge of systematizing our pedagogical experience of the training process lived with the participants of the Master in Robinsonian Education in the course Integral Human Development for Life (DHIPV) is to discuss, describe, reconstruct, explain the process lived and analyze the achievements and difficulties encountered by the students, bringing to light the new knowledge obtained during the experiences in order to achieve an integral relationship of being through the formation of a learning community that experiences: *knowing, knowing-being, knowing-how to do, knowing how to live together and knowing how to transcend* towards the Total Being. It is based on the dimensions of Education: *knowledge, experiences and values* and on the model of the Educated Being and Total Being (Legendre, 1995) and the consideration of the integrity of the being from the connections between *body, emotion, mind and spirit* (Chopra,1994, (Maturana, 1996, Legendre, 1995), the transformation in coexistence of Maturana (2000), the principles of an authentic educational theory Ceballos (2013), the spiritual of: Legendre (1995), Maturana, (2000), Walsh (2000), Tolle (2005), Maharishi Sadashiva Isham, (2006) among others. The methodology used was the systematization of experiences of the five "times" of Jara (2012): (1) The starting point: the experience; (2) Formulate a systematization plan; (3) The recovery of the lived process; (4) The background reflections and (5) The arrival points. The contribution of the course was the permanent and continuous evaluation of the educated self, through learning strategies such as: the portfolio and critical reflection of the experience, which allowed the analysis of the lived experience, of 47 testimonies, identifying the behavior of change through the achievement indicator: **realizing** in order to **take charge of**, and the observation criteria: *desire to change, respect for others, educating for life, conscious pedagogical practice, valuing the spiritual, and spiritual knowledge.* This made it possible to appreciate the daily life of personal and professional human contexts. The results reflected a significant impact on the achievement of individual and collective citizenship awareness among educators, providing the opportunity to acquire theoretical and practical tools for a healthy and prolonged life and the enjoyment of a horizon of dignified survival, with freedom, respect for oneself and others.

Keywords: teacher training, experiential mastery, educated self, total self, spirituality, Human Development.

DEDICATION

TO MY PARENTS...
Carmen (+) and Pedro (+) for their perseverance, advice and perseverance that characterized him... who enlighten me and fill my path with the fragrance of wild flowers to fulfill my dreams... *with love.*

TO GOD, THE MYSTICAL ROSE AND SAI BABA.
For having allowed me and facilitated the way to achieve my goal, *with infinite kindness and love.*

TO MY CHILDREN.
Eddy José and Eduardo, invaluable treasures, who accompany me in my dreams with understanding and fill my life with *joy and love* ...

TO MY HUSBAND.
Eddy is an unconditional companion at all times, a model of patience, support, companionship and *love.*

MY SIBLINGS, BROTHER-IN-LAW AND NIECES.
Irene, Pedro, Germán, Lismar, Jenny and Alexandra, stars that never cease to shine and shelter me with their *light and love.*

TO MY TEACHER.
Hilda, spiritual companion in the intellectual adventure in which we are vitally committed and united forever. *with love.*

TO MY PROFESSORS OF THE MASTER'S DEGREE IN ROBINSONIAN EDUCATION AND FACILITATORS OF THE DHIPV COURSE.
Those who made it possible to grow professionally and personally, fertilizing the ground of knowledge and experiences in the Educated Being until he/she became a Total Being *of love...*

TO THE BEACON OF LIGHT.
Who guides the sensitive souls, in the midst of the immeasurable sea, the sensitive beings who seek *light and love.*

THANK YOU

As a follower and inspirer to continue searching in our own theoretical-practical learning as a facilitator and companion in the teaching-learning process, I want to thank Dr. Mariñas and the Robinsonian Master's in Education for the space he gave me in the implementation of the Integral Human Development for Life course, which together with the guidance and construction of Dr. Beatriz Ceballos this experience germinated and I ventured to dialogue and take the risk and challenge of sharing it with you.

I owe the achievement of this new goal in my life to my spiritual sister Dr. Hilda Lokpez de George, for her concern, advice, encouragement, philosophy of life and support in my promotion work, who made possible the conception and completion of this work as well as my incorporation in a new field of systematization of experience, which turned out to be an academic adventure, and to MaE Berta Veitia de Morales, my permanent companion and critical friend who listened to me and reviewed the preliminary ideas embodied in the work.

To my friends and facilitators of the DHIPV course at the national level, especially Rosalia Morales and Coromoto Álvarez, who supported me with information about the experience in different nuclei and in the culmination of the work, for their words of encouragement and constant motivation to achieve this goal.

To all my participants of the Master's Degree in Robinsonian Education, especially to those who shared the experience of the course in the Apure, Maracay and San Juan de los Morros Nuclei for their unconditional support. Without them it would have been impossible to carry out this beautiful experience!

It is worth mentioning the support of Dr. Germán Cedeño, MaE. Irene Puertas and Dr. Silvia García, who provided me with relevant bibliography on the systematization of the experience and in the orientation of the quantitative data provided by the ECsA. Libertad Polanco.

To all those people who, in one way or another, gave me their collaboration. For everything and for everyone... A thousand thanks for such a beautiful Adventure and Dream Crystallized with love...

INTRODUCTION

Education is one of the fundamental pillars for the improvement of man in all areas. It also constitutes the support for each human being to satisfy his desire to learn to live, to become and to be and to be situated. The foundation of this approach is based on the consideration of the intimate relationship between the primary elements of being: body, emotion, language and spirit. That leads to human transformation in coexistence (Chopra, 1994, Maturana, 1996, Legendre, 1995, Ceballos, 2013).

In recent decades, popular and social movements have increased the actions of their community participation, educational and organizational processes, arising from the economic, social and political dynamics, all of these movements derive in the need to socialize, as stated by Jara (1998).

The challenge of our time is to achieve a world in which human beings can enjoy the freedom and autonomy to which we aspire and which we most strongly aspire.

This is precisely the challenge of Human Development, which during the 1990s made its way rapidly and strongly in the world, transforming the vision of national and local governments and international organizations on the ends and means of their action in the promotion of development.

In this sense, our reality faces a world of constant change and transformation, which affect the progress of our society, but at the same time the individual tends to be the main actor of his own history and his own human development, by providing the basis to act with autonomy and increase the opportunities to exercise it, so it should be given the importance required for the formation of the facilitator of own values, but also of information and learning skills to expand their life options and thus be able to raise the academic level and professional performance.

Integral human development for life is the process through which a society improves the conditions and quality of life of human beings in the environment in which they develop, in which the human rights of the facilitators are respected. It assumes the consideration of the integrity of the being from the connections between *body, emotion, mind and spirit, through* the development of the domains of the educated being: *cognitive-conceptual, emotional, physical, social, moral and perceptual* permanently integrated by the experiential domain that allows reaching the development of the spiritual dimension as the essence of human existence.

In this sense, it is expected that the personal development of the being, of oneself, of the other and of the community, implies self-knowledge, self-esteem, self-direction and self-efficacy, which leads to the deployment of their rational, emotional and spiritual potentialities, assume education as a way for social transformation and develop an ethics of educational action oriented by humanistic values with great sensitivity and social responsibility to a life of personal well-being, family, work and social well-being, whose purpose is to achieve a path of transformation, excellence and personal and professional transcendence to exercise a transformational leadership of the new century, within the framework of scientific, technological, socio-economic and spiritual advances.

All of the above, leads us to present the experience lived in the course Integral Human Development for Life (DHIPV) whose purpose was to achieve the integral development of the being through the formation of a learning community that experiences: *knowing, knowing-being, knowing-doing, knowing-how to live and knowing how to transcend towards the total being.* To provide the Robinsonian Magister with the idea of a good practice for the life of the development of human transformation supported by theoretical and methodological principles on human development that contributes to the formation of a professional with an individual and collective conscience towards his own transformation and of the quality of citizen education.

This Curricular Unit (DHIPV) was an exciting challenge, as was every activity carried out during the eight weeks planned, where the contents were oriented to *explore, experiment* and *experience* situations directly related to the development of the human being whose axiological integrating thematic axis was focused on

en: The integral formation of the being from the development of the educated being to the Total being and the

development of experiential mastery as a path to spiritual growth.

It is evident then, that this experience was an intense learning experience for the facilitators and participants of the course, in which we learned to respect the people with whom we worked, we learned to value their knowledge and knowledge produced in practice, we also learned to develop the sensitivity to carefully observe their experiences and testimonies, indicators such as: *awareness* in order to *take charge of,* and the criteria of: *desire to change, respect for others, educating for life, conscious pedagogical practice, valuing the spiritual* and *spiritual knowledge.*

The challenge is how to capture everything that happened in such a rich experience, how to collect, organize, understand, reconstruct and share in a systematic way what was experienced in the DHIPV course. For this, the methodology implemented by Jara (2012: pp. 161-197) was selected, with five "times": (1) The starting point: the experience; (2) Formulating a systematization plan; (3) The recovery of the lived process; (4) The background reflections and (5) The points of arrival, to systematize the experience.

Given this situation, it will be essential to share this experience with other people so that the main lessons learned not only remain with those who lived the practice and participated in the process, but also transcend the walls of the institution.

The contribution of the course was the permanent and continuous evaluation of the educated being, through the different learning strategies, such as: the portfolio, discussion forums, analysis of films and videos, readings, observation, experiential exercises and most importantly the permanent critical reflection of the experiences lived in the process, allowed the analysis of the lived and frequent situations, the construction of new knowledge and to value the daily life of the personal and professional human contexts.

The work presented is developed in six chapters.

In the first one, it is described: "The Methodological Horizon" where the origin and concept of systematization is developed, which we call: "This is how systematization was born and conceptualized", as well as the approach of eight principles of systematization, five epistemological approaches or supports and "this is how we will bundle it..." a methodological proposal. Taking into account the five "times" of Jara (2012). In the second and the successive ones, Jara's methodology is implemented. *The Starting Point*: The experience, where a historical account of the Master's Degree in Robinsonian Education is made, having participated in the experience, having records of it and proposal of the DHIPV course, presenting its description, justification, context, content, course activities, as well as the theoretical basis and the axes of Human Development that support the course. In the third part, a *Systematization Plan* is formulated and we ask ourselves: Why do we want to systematize? In this part we present the objectives of the systematization of the experience, then we develop What experience do we want to systematize? In other words, we define the object to be systematized, what are the central aspects of this experience that interest us? What sources of information do we have? Why do we want to systematize this experience? In the fourth part, which we call *Recovery of the Lived Process, in this* part we reconstruct, order and classify the information of the course. In the fifth chapter, *a Reflection on the Background* is made: why did what happened happen happen? where an analysis, synthesis and interpretation of the performance and of what was lived in the experience, both qualitatively and quantitatively, is made. Chapter six presents *the Points of Arrival*, that is, the conclusions, recommendations and strategies for communicating the lessons learned, and finally, the bibliographical references cited in the body of the work.

Chapter 1

1. METHODOLOGICAL HORIZON

> *2. By systematizing, people recover in an orderly way what they already know about their experience, discover what they do not yet know about it, but also reveal to them what they do not yet know that they already knew.*
>
> *Aravena, M and Zúñiga, C. (2002).*

2.1. - Thus was born and conceptualized... Systematization...

The origin and concept of systematization is not unknown, the only thing is that there is no agreement on the definition and origin of this strategy. Some authors such as the Alboan group (2008), Francke and Morgan (1995), Jara (2001) among others, point out that the opening of systematization began in the fifties, contextualized from the Academy of Social Sciences and Social Service in Latin America, and in the 1980s it was used in experiences of Popular Education in Costa Rica by Jara (2001) and from the School for Development in Lima, Francke and Morgan (1995) refer to in Peru, the first systematization proposals originated in the early 1980s, among different grassroots initiatives working in the methodological perspective of Popular Education. However, it is valid to recognize that organizing data in a "systematic" way is part of any scientific research process from the beginning. What is special and innovative about the "systematization" proposed in this period is the application of this process to *recover, organize, specify, clarify, reflect and contribute to* the knowledge of popular social activity and give it a scientific character.

It is important to note that in recent years, its most frequent uses have been associated, basically, with two fields:

- *The systematization of information or data systematization*: It is the ordering and classification of all types of data and information, under certain criteria, categories, relationships, with the objective of creating a database.
- *Systematization of experiences*: The experiences are described as a process that takes place in a given period of time, involving different actors, in an economic and social context and within the framework of a given institution.

In this paper we will refer to this second field as a methodological horizon.

In a first general approach, systematization is to increase our capacity to identify and organize relevant data on reality in order to transform it. Systematization is a very specific aspect of community action and of the organizers of community development programs. Although systematization is usually seen as a technical problem, it is also a political problem, since it is tied to the ultimate goals of educational action (Guzmán, 1991, p. 6).

The systematization of experiences is a participatory research methodology that involves real, historical, difficult processes when different actors are involved, and is carried out in a given economic-social context, Jara (2001). For the author, systematization means:

> ...a rigorous exercise of learning and critical interpretation of the processes experienced, which can make a decisive contribution to recreate the practices of social movements and to renew the theoretical production of the social sciences, from the daily experience of the peoples of Latin America, particularly those committed to processes of education and popular organization (Jara, 1994, p. 243).

Allowing the researcher:

> .to penetrate inside the dynamics of the experiences, something like getting inside these living and complex social processes, circulating among their elements, feeling the relationships among them, going through their different stages, locating their contradictions, tensions, marches and countermarches, thus coming to understand these processes from their own logic, extracting from there lessons that may contribute to the enrichment of both practice and theory (Jara, 2001, p. 165).

On the other hand, the author states that systematization is:

> ...a methodological process whose purpose is that the educator or promoter of a project recovers his/her relationship with the action, organizing what he/she knows about his/her practice in order to make it known to others (1987b) .it refers to a process through which what the subjects know about their experience is recovered, in order to be able to interpret it and then communicate it (1987c).

It should be noted that ten years earlier, Martinic, in Chile (1984a, cited by Jara, 2012, p.66) states that the systematization of experience is:

> .a process of reflection that aims to order or organize the progress, processes and results of a project, seeking in such dynamics the dimensions that can explain the course taken by the work carried out.(p.4) As the experience involves several authors, systematization also tries to elucidate the sense or meaning that the process has had for the main actors in it.

Within this order of ideas, Verger (2003, p.2), maintains that the systematization of experiences is:

> .the process of reconstruction and analytical reflection on an action or intervention experience in order to interpret and understand it. a consistent knowledge is obtained that allows the experience to be transmitted, confronted with other experiences or with existing theoretical knowledge.

Pischeda, quoted by Pierola (1999, p. 72), states that systematization should aim to be:

.a reflective process oriented in a frame of reference and with a work method that allows us to organize an analysis of the experience that gives an account of what we do, that facilitates communication, and that makes us aware of what we have done. In other words, when we speak of systematization, Jara (2012, p. 64) states that

.we are referring to historical processes in which all these different elements are concatenated in a permanent dynamism and interdependence, continuously producing changes and transformations.

In this process of building a critical and participatory knowledge, where we discover and weave plots of meaning of our experience, systematization, as Selener, (1996, p. 7) says "is a methodology that facilitates the description, reflection, analysis and documentation, in a continuous and participatory manner, of processes and results of a development project".

Through systematization it is possible to problematize and identify individual and group conflicts and contradictions, since it is a process where the development of a specific experience is organized, articulated, reflected, produced and socialized.

Systematization is a process that records, describes, reflects, analyzes, organizes and communicates the development of an experience or project. Each of these steps or elements are interrelated and linked to a community project (Medina, 1994, p. 22).

In the same vein, Barrera (2010, p.17) argues that the systematization of experience consists of:

The research activity aimed at presenting in an organized, coherent and efficient manner experiences, situations or practices, susceptible of becoming scientific contributions, based on the specification of their processes, experiences, theoretical development and contributions, which merits a work of analysis and subsequent abstraction.

In these twelve (12) definitions of different authors (Jara, 1989, 1994 and 2001); Martinic (1984); Guzman, 1991; Pischeda, (cited by Pierola, 1999); Selener, D. and others (1996); Medina (1994): Verger (2003) and Barrera (2010), there are some common elements. On the one hand, they propose critical, analytical, practical, rational and scientific reflection, which requires the researcher, who will carry out the systematization, to ask a series of questions about the experience: What was done? Why was it done? Why was it done in this way and not in another? What results were obtained? What were these results useful for? Who were they useful to?

And on the other hand, the twelve definitions raise the idea of organizing, ordering: practices, knowledge, ideas, experiences, data, etc., which until then were scattered and which will be fundamental to reconstruct the practice. And finally, the aim is to discover, transmit, confront or explain the logic and the course of the work carried out.

In this order of ideas, Martinic's (1987) sentences are revealing. He shows that "... interpretations of systematization are permeated by different conceptions and practices...". And they also allow inferring that the debate about it will still have to go a long way. He also maintains that "systematization aims at achieving a knowledge that is neither alien nor opposed to experience", stressing that "it is not a simple abstraction and generalization of already accumulated knowledge, but an organized reading". Of a conscious reading of practice and its interrelation with reality (Martinic, cited in Pierola, 1999, p.71).

Systematization emphasizes the development of processes. Vergar (2002, p. 4) states that those who systematize are interested in rescuing the process, showing how it has been carried out, analyzing the effects of the intervention on the subjects and the nature of the relationships that have been generated. "It allows the construction of a common vision of the experience among those who have participated in it: successes, errors, limits and possibilities".

In short, the author adds that systematization enables stakeholders to give meaning to their actions, to adopt a privileged position for the interpretation of the experiences in which they participate, to observe them in an integral and complete way, to share this view with other stakeholders and to have more elements to know what the next steps should be.

The definition of systematization varies according to the purpose for which the process is carried out and is permanently connected to evaluation, planning, organization and self-management. It is a process that involves ordering and describing coherently and objectively the events and knowledge of subjects located in a historical, contextual and socio-political space (Garcés, 1988, p. 6).

In view of the above, Fajardo, quoted by Pierola (1999, p.71) states that systematization is a synthesis of "empirical and conceptual antecedents that make it possible to explain the scope and meaning of popular education practices". Thus emphasizing the interrelation between theory and practice, between what is formulated and what is carried out; that is, a process of explanatory evaluation.

In essence, systematization reconstructs daily practice, in a "here and now", analyzing one's own records or the information obtained in the experience, in order to produce knowledge through follow-up and reflection on what was done in practice, and to advance and improve future intervention projects (Kisnerman and Mustieles, 1999, p.7).

Systematization is a process through which the subjects recover what they know about their experience in order to understand, interpret and communicate it, thus producing a new type of knowledge Martinic and Walker, (1987, p. 9)

For the scope of the interpretations, it is important to prioritize the phenomena, and subsequently make judgments that allow their socialization and valuation in order to influence reality.

It is worth considering that Ghiso (1998) values systematization as a heuristic procedure, since, based on the method of reflection, discourses and actions are analyzed in order to discover those situations that limit decisions and effective practices. This makes systematization a conscious process that captures the meanings of action and its consequences, where the organization of experiences and the theories implicit in them, contextualize praxis and communicate knowledge.

Similarly, Quiróz and Morgan (1988) consider systematization as a research process because: (a) as a method of analysis it can recover the knowledge implicit in the experiences; (b) it can "generate social knowledge from the experiences to offer it as orientation to other similar experiences" (p. 53); (c) it generalizes from the information it analyzes; and (d) it communicates and disseminates the knowledge.

Lókpez de George (1994, p.12) considers systematization as a process that: (a) organizes information; (b) constructs experience; (c) evaluates and (d) proposes actions for the improvement of the experience. According to this definition, the function of systematization is to organize information in a systematic way and/or historical recovery of the experience, through the reflection of both collective and individual practice. In any case, the fundamental purpose is to reach "(a) the construction/reconstruction of the experience; (b) the construction/reconstruction of the experience, its evaluation and proposal of action for its improvement." (p. 13).

The author points out that systematization:

> is carried out from two perspectives: one retrospective, aimed at the description, analysis and evaluation of the experiences, and the other, as a continuous process within group learning, in which individual and collective projects are analyzed and fed back by the participants (p. 13).

In this way it can be argued that systematization builds and produces new forms of thoughts and technologies on the methodological basis of reflection and critique.

Thus, on the basis of what has been discussed above, the following characteristics and usefulness of systematization can be pointed out:

1.   Systematization *is preceded by a practice,* which can be recovered and recontextualized from the knowledge acquired.

2.   In systematization, every action, subject or context *generates knowledge.*

3.   Systematization *is a process of interlocution* between people, "in which discourses, theories and cultural constructions are negotiated" (Ghiso, 1998, p. 6).

4.   As a knowledge-building process, systematization *is not neutral*; the interest it orients

is emancipatory (Carr and Kemmis, 1995).

5.   It builds knowledge with *socio-critical proposals*. In systematization, *both the process and the product* are important.

6.   In systematization, *formative processes* are *generated*. "We are talking here about highly significant learning for those who participate" (Ghiso, 1998, p. 6).

7.   Systematization allows us to *learn* critically from educational practice, to *reflect* on the *experience* and thus be able to: (a) improve our own practice and transform it; (b) share the lessons learned with other similar experiences and (c) contribute to the enrichment of theory and the construction of collective theory and practices (Jara, 2001).

8.   An instrument that facilitates the professional of the *action*, the *organization* of *knowledge* produced during *practice*, its contrast with what he/she knew beforehand and with the accumulated knowledge (theory), and the production of useful lessons and learning to guide new practices (Barnechea, González and Morgan, 1998, p. 9).

9.   Methodology of *inquiry expos*, which takes social practice as an object of problematization and knowledge production, to describe, characterize and conceptualize phenomena associated with social problems in their micro social expression (Clemente, 1997).

10.   Systematization encompasses a set of activities aimed at *ordering, classifying, analyzing and interpreting* the *contents and results of praxis* in an organized manner (Evia and Gudynas, 1993, p. 263).

11.   Systematization involves contrasting the initial project with the results achieved, thus contributing to: (a) the presentation of the experiences, (b) the organization and socialization of the work and (c) the assumption of the reality or experiences as a premise.

12.   It is a process that: (a) organizes information; (b) constructs experience; (c) evaluates and (d) proposes actions to improve the experience (Lókpez de George, 1994, p. 12).

13.   Contributes to improving strategies, approaches and methodologies.

14.   Provide feedback on the interventions of the teams and the institution.

15.   It favors the professional development of the teams and the institution.

16.   Contribute documentation to the institution's comprehensive information system.

17.   Support for own production of new technologies and new knowledge based on experience.

18.   The technologies and knowledge generated can be applied and useful in other contexts, as well as generate alliances with other organizations and institutions. (from 14 to 18 were taken from the Regional Workshop on Planning, Monitoring and Evaluation of the SPFS, September 2003. Guatemala)

In view of the above, we found different interpretations that ratify at the same time the existence of common elements as component factors of systematization. It is not our intention to homogenize and much less to unify what is understood by systematization, since we believe that in diversity lies the richness of the process, of a concept to be defined; we set forth some of the definitions that we have found in the documents reviewed.

For the purposes of this work, systematization is conceptualized with the elements incorporated in the characteristics and utilities that we exposed previously where we allow ourselves and risk defining it *as a formative, critical and reflective process of the educational and technological practice that allows us to order, classify, analyze and interpret the events experienced through a recoverable and reconstructive practice that favors the personal and professional development of the educated being and to be able to share the experience with other people.*

1.1.1.- Principles of Systematization

In systematization, seven principles proposed by Selener (1996) and the eighth incorporated by Lókpez de George (2009) should be considered: Selener, (1996) and the eighth incorporated by Lókpez de George (2009), since they allow guiding the process of reconstruction of experiences. These principles are the following: (1) Relevance and necessity (2) Comprehensiveness or Globality (3) Historical perspective (4) Relativity of information (5) Plurality of opinions and knowledge (6) Use of local and scientific knowledge (7) Participation and finally, (8) Ethical behavior, all of which are shown in the following table.

Box 1: Eight principles of systematization

1.	**Relevance and Necessity:** it is perceived as useful and necessary by all the stakeholders.
2.	actors/authors **Integrality or Comprehensiveness:** the project analysis should be carried out considering
3.	the broad social context: social, economic, political, cultural and other aspects. **Historical perspective:** consider historical roots and current trends.
4.	**Relativity of the information**: actions taken and lessons learned
5.	may be relevant to a particular situation or to those with similar characteristics. **Plurality of opinions and knowledge:** reality is interpreted in different ways.
	The systematization process is enriched by factors such as culture, education, gender and age. This enriches the systematization process.

6.	**Use of local and scientific knowledge:** both local and scientific knowledge is collected.
7.	**Participation:** The description and analysis of the project should be done in a participatory manner, taking into account all points of view.
8.	**Ethical behavior*:** guided by ethical principles of integrity, respect for the dignity and rights of persons, solidarity, justice, equity, co-responsibility. Using ethical principles of research: informed consent, voluntary participation, right to privacy, confidentiality and anonymity, protection from harm.

Note: Information taken from Selener, D. (1996) Documenting, evaluating and learning from our development projects. Manual de Sistematización Participativa. Quito: International Institute for Rural Reconstruction (IIRR).

* This last principle was added by Dr. Hilda Lókpez de George.

1.1.2. - Systematization Approaches

In systematization processes, the analysis and study of reality require a posture that orients the historical construction of experiences and discourses; this posture must be determined: (a) by the conception of the nature of the experience to be systematized (b) by the relations that the systematizer has with what is systematized and (c) by the way in which knowledge is constructed from practice.

Ghiso (1998, p.12) differentiates between the different systematization proposals, stating that "if we recognize that there is a diversity of subjects and therefore of logics and rationalities, cultures and discourses that lead to the reflection and expression of knowledge built in relation to practices, we can, then, assume that there are *different epistemological supports"* and points out that there are five systematization approaches:

1. *Historical-dialectical approach*: In which experiences are part of a general social and historical practice, equally dynamic, complex and contradictory, which can be read and understood dialectically, understanding them as a rich and contradictory unit, full of constituent elements that are in constant movement. These practices are related to other similar practices in contexts that allow them to be explained (Jara, 1994).

2. *Dialogic and interactive approach:* In which experiences are understood as spaces of interaction, communication and relationship; they can be read from the language that is spoken and in the social relationships established in these contexts. In this approach, it is important to build knowledge based on external and internal referents that allow to thematize the problematic areas expressed in the conversational processes that occur in every social practice. The keys are: to recognize all action as a dialogic space, to relate dialogue and context, that is, to introduce the problem of power and communicative control devices,

recognizing in the different situations the elements that organize, coordinate and condition interaction (Martinic, 1996). In systematizations developed from this perspective, categories such as: context units, thematic nuclei, actor's perspectives, actor's categories, meaning units, cognitive and structural mediations are also usually used.

3. *Hermeneutic approach: This* approach takes into consideration the need to understand the actors of sociocultural and educational projects in the development of reflexive practical reasons, through a series of processes that make explicit and make clear: intentions, predispositions, hypotheses, meanings and evaluations that underlie the action (Osorio, 1998). It is from this approach that systematization is understood as an interpretative work of all those who participated, revealing the games of meaning and the dynamics that allow reconstructing the relationships between the actors, the knowledge and the processes of legitimacy, that is, to account for the cultural density of the experience. From this approach it is stated: *"we systematize experiences, that is, interpretations of an event, from the sociocultural thickness of each of the participants"* (Hleap, 1995).

4. *Approach of reflexivity and the construction of human experience:* These approaches assume the implicit epistemology of practice, based on the observation and analysis of problems that have no place in the learned or applied theoretical body. Systematization is linked here to problem solving, allowing to face the new challenges presented by the context. Systematization thus seeks to recover tacit knowledge, which is implicit in the action guidelines, in the perception of the problem faced. The knowledge, judgments and skills that are intangible in the action are recognized and valued. In this type of process it is discovered that, by recovering and reflecting on the experience, the subject recognizes himself observing, speaking and acting, and this allows him to separate the experience from its logic of explanation, in the very act of understanding and explaining it (Pakman, 1996). (Pakman, 1996).

5. *Deconstructive approach:* From this approach, systematization could be understood as an intervention that allows entering into the voice, into the self-consciousness of the institutional, into the imaginaries and into those fields where there are institutionalized forms of exercising power. It is a listening to the margins of the institutional machinery, suspecting everything that is claimed to be working well. Knowledge is constructed by recognizing the traces left by action and the origins of action, since these never disappear. From this perspective, the epistemological condition is that of uncertainty that propitiates throughout the systematization process the generation of questions that place the actors in the possibility of abandoning what they are, to place themselves in a horizon of construction of what they

can be (Mejía, 1989).

6. The above only wants to show that different approaches to systematization may exist as a result of theoretical-practical closures; but it must also be recognized that there are hybridizations among them. As was said in the 1980s: "Interpretations of systematization are permeated by different conceptions and practices, which suggests that the debate on systematization will have a long way to go" (Aporte 32, 1989). (Contribution 32, 1989).

For this work, the fourth approach "*reflexivity and the construction of human experience*" was taken as a tool that would complement and nurture the methodological proposal of the program of a course of the Master's Degree in Robinsonian Education of the Universidad Nacional Experimental Simón Rodríguez called: *Integral human development for life,* this choice is due to the fact that the central purpose of the course is to achieve the integral development of the *being through* the formation of a learning community that experiences ways to influence *knowledge, know-being, know-doing, know-how to live, know how to create and know how to transcend* towards the *total being,* since as Barnechea, Gonzalez and Morgan, (1998, p.10), the systematization of experience guides professionals and/or researchers to "give order and rigor to the knowledge that is in their practice".

1.2. - And so we will do it... a methodological proposal

Oscar Jara's (2012) proposal on what method to use, what steps to take, what techniques to use, etc., reflects that there are no rigid protocols, but a multiplicity of possibilities. What we do have to be clear about are the **criteria and** methodological **principles** that will enable us to "structure a whole work "strategy": planning, designing, executing orderly and coherent processes that have a logical cumulative sequence and result in a *qualitative transformation* of the situation from which they started" (p. 163).

These criteria must be taken into account in two ways:

1 - The overall sequence of the process, which must ensure that it has overall coherence as a whole.

2 -The tools, which can be almost infinite and for each moment of the process (to make records, historical recovery, analysis, synthesis, communication, socialization).

In any case, Jara (2012) stresses that we must not lose sight of the integrality of the process: that each tool used serves to achieve the overall vision and objective. We should not be captivated by fashionable techniques or by one that we like the most, but "be open to what happens along the way in order to modify its course if necessary, to the extent that those who propose the path are, in turn, walkers" (ob, cit. p. 164). This means that we must be able to use a whole "logic of the process" that we want to promote, and give unity to all the factors that acted, in our case: the participants of the DHIPV course, their personal and group characteristics, their needs, their interests, the context in which the course was lived, their knowledge about the subject, the course objectives to be achieved, the different stages they developed in the two Modules, the thematic sequence they followed in the four Learning Guides, the techniques and procedures used in the different moments, the practical application tasks that were proposed and carried out to culminate the course.

For didactic reasons, Jara (2012, pp. 165-166) suggests as a proposal "in five times" the systematization of experiences, which we will take into consideration this method to implement our educational practice in the Integral Human Development for Life course.

The five "Times

(1)   The starting point: Experience

(2)   Formulate a systematization plan

(3)   Recovery of the lived process

(4)   The underlying reflection and

(5)   Arrival points.

Each "time" has, in turn, some constituent moments (or elements), which are presented below:

1 The starting point: The experience.

(a)   *To have participated in the experience through* what we do, what we feel and what we think.

(b)   *To have records of the experiences.* It is a matter of starting from the practice itself. "...only *those who have been part of* an experience can systematize it" (p.167), i.e., for systematization to be real and effective, it must be carried out by setting the actors themselves in motion.

2 Formulate a systematization plan.

(a)   *Why do we want to systematize?* (Define the purpose of this systematization)

(b)   *What experience(s) do we want to systematize?* (Delimit the object to be systematize)

(c)   *What central aspects of this experience are of most interest to you?* systematization axis?

(d)   *What sources of information do we have/need?*

(e)   *What procedures will we follow?*

It is necessary to define as clearly as possible the meaning, the usefulness, the product that is expected to be obtained from the systematization and what central aspects of these experiences we are interested in systematizing. In our case, we are going to present the practice of the participants who lived the DHIPV course in a concrete, clear way and give meaning and usefulness to the process and product that took place in the aforementioned experience.

3 Recovery of the lived process

(a)   *Reconstruct the history of the experience.* At this point we must have a global and chronological vision of the principles and events that took place during the experience through records, whether photos, videos, or the creation of portfolios.

(b)   *Sorting and classifying the information.* This phase allows us to accurately reconstruct the different aspects of the experience seen as a process. Actions, results, intentions and the different opinions of both those who promote the experience and those who participate in it must be taken into account.

It is a matter of reconstructing the history of the practice in the period that has been indicated (delimitation of the object). These are the main facts, actions and events that took place during that time; records are used and arranged in chronological order.

It is important to draw a parallel chronology of the main significant events, and a tool is extremely useful to organize and articulate the information about the experience around the basic aspects that interest us.

4 Background reflection

(a)   *Analysis and synthesis process*

(b)   *Critical interpretation*

To analyze, synthesize and critically interpret the lived process, **why did what happened happen happen, we** must try to go beyond the descriptive, to carry out an orderly process of abstraction to find the raison d'être of what happened in the experience. That is why the key question of this "time" is: Why did what happened happen?

Through the analysis, synthesis and critical interpretation of the process, we identify the main tensions or contradictions that have arisen, and finally, concepts will be established.

It is recommended to make a guide of critical questions about the process of the experience that allows to identify the essential factors that have intervened and to make explicit the logic and sense of the experience.

5 Arrival points

(a)   *Formulate conclusions.* This is the last stage of this methodological proposal. All reflection should result in the formulation of theoretical, methodological and practical conclusions.

(b)   *Communicating the lessons learned.* A material will be produced to communicate what has been learned and learned in the systematization of the experience.

Chapter 2

II. THE STARTING POINT: EXPERIENCE

*...we have **to start from** what we do, what we feel and what we think...*
putting the actors themselves in motion.

Jara, Oscar, 1999

II.1. History of the Master's Degree in Robinsonian Education [1]

The Master's Program in Robinsonian Education was designed in 2006 with the purpose of raising the academic level and professional performance of UNESR facilitators in accordance with the strategic guidelines of the Development Plan of the Simón Bolívar Nation (MPPCI, 1999).

In this sense, they are expected to develop their rational, emotional and spiritual potential, to assume education as a means for social transformation and to develop an ethic of educational action guided by humanistic values with great sensitivity and social responsibility.

In the order of the previous ideas, the educational fact is assumed from a collective, bioethical, ecopolitical and spiritual dimension; and therefore, it is oriented to strengthen an eco-awareness, a transdisciplinary, ecologizing and dialogic knowledge, designing a new educational discourse that claims from a theory of feeling the educational praxis of the Robinsonian magister. All this with an emerging vision of education that implies the possibility of rethinking it from alternative paradigms, which are oriented towards "a new way of being, doing and knowing" of the Society of the XXI century.

Indeed, it is expected that the participant's contact with alternative educational experiences will allow him/her to configure a path of knowledge that will serve as a basis to problematize from a holistic and integral vision and make possible his/her participation in the transformation of his/her reality as an active social subject. This new educational practice leads us to reflect on the andragogic paradigm and turn our gaze to critical cosmovisions in an attempt to unite theoretical thought with practical action and somehow prefigure the educational circumstances of our present and the importance of sensitivity in human thought, whose absences have resulted in the loss of feelings of identity, of ethics and civic responsibility, of the disarticulation of cohesion and solidarity.

---

[1] UNESR. (2006) Institutional Document. Postgraduate Dean's Office. Diseño curricular de la Maestría en Educación Robinsoniana. Caracas. Autor.

In this context, the program will promote the creation of conditions for:

a) human transformation
b) the democratization and collectivization of knowledge to reach all areas of the national reality
c) the de-schooling of education through the exploration of new ways of knowing and learning
d) reconceptualization of the roles of teacher, student, citizen and authority.
e) the rescue of the emancipatory role of the "robinsonian master".
f) recognition of the diversity, plurality and richness of multiple learning environments.
g) the new ecology of self-employment, free from all forms of exploitation and slavery
h) the development of research projects inspired by a critical-endogenous social research for university transformation from the communities.

We consider that the formation of a new "republican" as wisely proposed by Simón Rodríguez, would not be possible if, together with changes of an educational, organizational and ideological nature, the conditions for the unfolding of human potentialities in the field of spirituality are not included.

Therefore, this master's degree promotes the conditions that allow the unfolding of human potential, ethical behavior, spontaneous creativity and collective conscience in its participants, based on a humanistic, transforming, emancipating education that is definitely opposed to an education based on competition and individualistic values. Consequently, it is necessary to deepen critical reflection, emotionality and spirituality as the prevailing rationality of a human education, in order to generate new ways of being, doing, knowing and living together.

The program is offered under the modality of supervised distance studies, defined in the Regulations on the Regime of Studies of the UNESR (1989) as a periodic interaction between the participant and his facilitators, with guidance for the fulfillment of learning activities by the participant, based on the principles of distance education and aimed at guiding the participant towards the search, acquisition and construction of knowledge and towards the development of skills, abilities, attitudes, values and behaviors through different techniques that allow his progressive independence during the process of education and training. (Articles 37 and 40 of the Regulations on the Regime of Studies of the UNESR).

For the Master's Degree in Robinsonian Education, this modality foreseen in the regulations is complemented by the quality of being administered "online" given that the fulfillment of learning activities planned and self-managed by the participant, are carried out using instructional materials managed on a technological platform and other materials that are designed and oriented by the course coordinator.

Therefore, admission to the Master's Degree in Robinsonian Education stipulates a basic training aimed at the knowledge and management of the technological platform and for the development of basic digital skills, which guarantee both the participant and the facilitator the construction of the minimum bases for a successful transition in the program. To this end, facilitators are expected to participate in continuous training spaces that seek to promote their updating in the technological area and in the model of online supervised studies proposed by UNESR, as well as the unification of the andragogical criteria present in the learning and evaluation processes of the program.

In this sense, the training activities planned under this modality foresee 80% of their development in a Moodle virtual platform (Version 1.7 +) which is accessed from the geographical location of each participant, while the remaining 20% corresponds to face-to-face activities that are carried out at the headquarters of the twenty-two UNESR centers located nationwide; this is done in two (2) face-to-face meetings and workshops at the beginning and at the end of the course.

The identification of the transversal axes of the Master's design was based on the proposals generated in a collective construction workshop held in March 2007 with the participation of teachers, students, administrative personnel, and directors of UNESR, as well as a group of teachers and students from other universities in the country.

In this context, and as a result of the work of reflection and participatory construction of the curriculum, six transversal axes emerged that give dynamism and integrality to the different components of the curriculum in this Master's program. *Socio-community research, 2. Environment and Sustainability, 3. Technology and Society, 4. National and Latin American Identity, 5. Popular and Emancipatory Education, and 6.-Human Transformation* (UNESR, 2006, p. 22).

The axis we are concerned with is that of human transformation, as an important requirement in the realization of the Integral Human Development for Life course.

This process of change requires three fundamental considerations, as outlined in the design of the Robinsonian Master's in Education:

1. To replace the bureaucratic organizational structures that today govern the management of the socio-economic activity of the country, with a new organization capable of empowering the popular bases through structures that generate autonomy in the operative bases of the organizations.

2. Total collectivization of education as a runway for the take-off and development of Venezuelans, possible only through the intensive use of information and communication technologies.

3. A human transformation oriented to the formation of an integral human being with a collective conscience capable of establishing new interaction relationships with his peers (UNESR, 2006, p. 28).

Likewise, for the approach of this axis we consider three dimensions: Development of the human being in the emotional and spiritual spheres; Education for life and social organization (Ob cit. p.29).

In this sense, the formation of a new "republican", as Simón Rodríguez wisely proposed, will not be possible if, together with the educational, organizational and ideological changes that this master's degree proposes, a new way of understanding human beings that includes all their potentialities: reason, emotion and spirit, is not conceived in the context.

Thus, the course "*Integral Human Development for Life*" (DHIPV) provides the Master's degree participant with the opportunity to acquire practical tools for a healthy, prolonged life and the enjoyment of a horizon of dignified survival, with freedom and self-respect. Based on the World Report on Human Development 1990-2011, which defined human development as "a process that gives people greater opportunities" and emphasizes the freedom of human beings to have health, education and enjoy fuller living conditions. But it also emphasizes that human development and well-being are much more than the sum of these dimensions and translate into a broader range of capabilities, including political freedom, human rights and, as Adam Smith said, "the ability to interact with others without being ashamed to appear in public". (quoted in United Nations Development Program (2011, p.1).

For this reason, this master's degree includes the axis of Human Transformation to investigate, within the framework of scientific, technological, socio-economic and spiritual advances, the possible deployment of human potentialities from theoretical and practical experiences based on the contributions to knowledge that humanity has generated on this subject. We believe that the rescue of human potentialities and the liberation of collective energy is a possible way to reach the holistic vision of a social being harmonized with its spirituality.

II.2. Have participated in the experience and have records of the experience.

The course Integral Human Development for Life is part of the curricular matrix of the Master's program in Robinsonian Education, in the component of deepening, a mandatory course with 2 credit units; it is a distance course offered at national level whose headquarters is the Regional Postgraduate Center of Caracas located in the Piloña Building, Francisco Solano López Avenue, intersection with Pascual Navarro Street, Sabana Grande Urb.

Additionally, its administration is supported by the human and infrastructure resources of the

Center for Educational Innovation and Technology (CITE) and the Postgraduate Dean's Office of the Universidad Nacional Experimental Simón Rodríguez, both located in the Metropolitan Area of Caracas. For this reason, the entire design and administration process is the responsibility of the three aforementioned entities.

The course program: "Integral Human Development for Life" (DHIPV) is proposed under my coordination, between March-September 2009 and 2010, at the request of the rector Dr. Manuel Mariñas, in September 2008, the design of the DHIPV course program is carried out jointly with Dr. Beatriz Ceballos and Maritza Puertas.

We were asked to prepare the program, advise on the design, as well as to participate and train the team of facilitators (Rosalía Morales, Carmen Suárez, Coromoto Álvarez, Sonia Carrillo, Sara Rodríguez, Hilda Dos Santos) to be distributed in 23 nuclei and the Santa Fe, El Valle and IDECYT headquarters, as shown in Table 2. These nuclei and headquarters were grouped into 5 zones and 2 regions, as presented in Table 3.

Table 2: Distribution of sites and nuclei of participants enrolled in the Master's Degree in Robinsonian Education and their respective facilitators and responsible persons. Period May-July 2009- I

Name of the site or Nucleus	No. of Enrollees	Facilitators	Responsible
Apure Nucleus	25	Maritza Puertas	Kristal Mujica
Araure Nucleus	32	Sonia Carrillo	Arturo Jimenez
Barcelona Center	17	Coromoto Alvarez	Leonor Ortega
Caricuao Center	2	Rosalia Morales	Richard Toro
Barquisimeto Center	12	Coromoto Alvarez	Ronald Ordóñez
Ciudad Bolivar Center	6	Coromoto Alvarez	Juan Sarmiento
Core Choir	12	Coromoto Alvarez	Keila Arevalo
Canoabo Nucleus	18	Carmen Suarez	Gilberto Toro Nirva Mendoza (E)
CEPAP Core	3	Rosalia Morales	---
Núcleo El Vigía	26	Carmen Suarez	Norelis Duque
Núcleo La Grita	15	Rosalia Morales	Hectilma Ruiz J
Name of the site or Nucleus	**No. of Enrollees**	**Facilitators**	**Responsible**
Núcleo Los Teques	13	Carmen Suarez	Kety Bautista (E)
Maracay Center	19	Beatriz Ceballos	Carmen Gonzalez
Maturín Center	27	Hilda Dos Santos	Gregorio A.Cermeño

Postgraduate Center Caracas	14	Rosalia Morales	---
Palo Verde Nucleus	43	Hilda Dos Santos	Juan B. Hernandez
San Carlos Center	27	Sara Rodriguez	Julio C. Camejo R
Santa Fe Headquarters	2	Rosalia Morales	---
San Juan de los Morros Center	26	Maritza Puertas	Juan C. Prado C. Darmary Armas
Valles del Tuy Center	21	Carmen Suarez	Richard Castro
Valera Center	31	Rosalia Morales	Alexis Rojas
Easter Valley Center	4	Hilda Dos Santos	Hector Rodriguez
Zaraza Nucleus	20	Sonia Carrillo	Rodolfo Salazar
El Valle Headquarters, Idecyt	1	Rosalia Morales	---
Mucuchíes Nucleus	6	Rosalia Morales	---
TOTAL	422	8	22

Source: Data provided by Control de Estudio. Postgraduate Dean's Office. Coordination of the Master's Degree in Robinsonian Education, 2009. Academic Period 2009-I. Caracas. Own elaboration

Table 3: Distribution of participants enrolled in the Integral Human Development for Life course according to regions and zones in the 2009-I academic period (May-July 2009).

AREAS AND REGIONS	REGISTERED
Greater Caracas Zone (Palo Verde and Central Department)	65
Altos Mirandinos Zone (Los Teques, Valles del Tuy)	34
Oriente Region (Barcelona, Ciudad Bolívar, Maturín, Valle de la Pascua and Zaraza)	74
Western Zone (Araure, San Carlos)	59
South Zone (Apure)	25
Western South Zone (Barquisimeto, Coro)	24
Central Zone (Canoabo, Maracay, San Juan de los Morros)	63
Andean Region (La Grita, Valera, El Vigía and Mucuchíes)	78
TOTAL	422

Source: Data provided by Control de Estudio. Postgraduate Dean's Office. Coordination of the Master's Degree in Robinsonian Education, 2009. Academic Period 2009-I. Caracas. Own elaboration

The DHIPV course proposes a new educational essay inspired by the contributions of valuable thinkers (Simón Rodríguez, Pietro Figueroa, Paulo Freire, among others) to the reconstruction of a new social order that makes possible the subjectivation, the realization and the necessary transformation of education.

Thus, this course in its educational vision is based on the postulates of critical humanism, social constructivism and a conception of the human being that integrates emotionality, spirituality and rationality as the central pivot that will generate changes and develop the potential of each person, in the search for a more just society and an authentic approach to communities.

II.3. Integral Human Development for Life Course Proposal

II.3.1- *Course description*

The curricular unit called "*Integral Human Development for Life*" is of great importance for the academic formation of the Master in Robinsonian Education.

The general purpose of the course is to provide the Robinsonian Magister with the idea of the development of Human Transformation supported by theoretical and methodological principles on human development that contributes to the formation of a professional with an individual, collective and citizen awareness towards their own transformation and the quality of education. This approach coincides with the proposal of one of the indispensable processes of change to achieve social transformation, according to Mariña (2008), the unfolding of the knowledge of the spirituality of each person.

The personal development of the *self, of oneself, of the other and of the community*, implies self-knowledge, self-esteem, self-direction and self-efficacy, which leads to a life of personal, family, work and social well-being, whose purpose is to achieve a path of transformation, excellence and personal and professional transcendence to exercise a transformational leadership of the new century, within the framework of scientific, technological, socio-economic and spiritual advances.

Succeeding or being successful has been the goal of human beings when starting any life project, which is why its development in recent decades has achieved an important and transcendental position; authors such as Legendre, 1995; Maturana, 1997b; Ceballos, 2008; Walsh, 2000; Tolle, 2005; Dyer, 2001; MSI (1996); Chopra, 1994, make contributions on how to achieve a whole and complete being who can successfully carry out everything he undertakes.

It has been proven that if we care about achieving the quality of life we desire, all the activities we perform will be carried out in a climate of trust, communication and freedom, interacting with less stress; obtaining productive and healthy results.

The *Integral Human Development for Life* Curricular Unit provides good practices for a healthy life oriented to explore, experiment and experience situations directly related to the development of the human being.

In this sense, the objective is to form a learning community that experiences ways to influence *knowledge, know-being, know-how, know-how to do, know-how to live together, know how to create and know how to transcend* towards the *total being.*

II.3.2- Justification

This curricular unit constitutes a basic factor within the human transformation of the preparation, formation and training of a new "republican", who visualizes himself with all his potentialities: reason, emotion and spirit (UNESR, 2006).

For this reason, this curricular unit intends to establish as a proposal, the good practices of healthy living and the development of Human Transformation supported by theoretical and methodological principles that contribute to the formation of a professional with an individual and collective conscience towards educational transformation.

It assumes the consideration of the integrity of the being from the connections between *body, emotion, mind and spirit*, through the development of the **domains of the educated being**: cognitive-conceptual, *emotional, physical, social, moral, perceptual,* permanently integrated by the **experiential domain** that allows reaching the development of the *spiritual dimension* as the essence of human existence.

Consequently, this theoretical-practical course is developed by involving the participants directly and actively, so that they make significant contributions derived from their experiences of real situations, previous experiences, the readings done on each topic and the situation of interactive experiences with peers and experts as part of the process of helping a real case, as this is considered one of the fundamental tools of the participant and Robinsonian facilitator.

II.3.3- Context of the proposal and course activities:

The Integral Human Development for Life course is offered as a learning space in order to contribute to the participants' desire to *learn to be, to become and to situate themselves.* The nature of the course, already described in the program, with a fundamental weight on the experiential domain, demands a module design that promotes the development and expansion of this domain among the participants.

We define the scope in the following terms:

Self-observation and expansion of the inner world for its translation into more satisfactory spaces of action, attending to the different elements of the human being: *corporal, emotional, mental, spiritual and the domains of the educated being/total being.*

- The integration of human formation in the different environments: *family, school, university and community.*

Two modules are proposed, each with two learning guides, where the activities developed, readings and the evaluation to be followed in the development of the course are graphed and attached at the end of the work.

First module: "The integral formation of the being from the development of the educated being to the Total Being" (See Graph 2 and Annex A).

Second module: "The development of the experiential domain of the educated being as a path to spiritual growth". (See graph 3 and annex B)

II.3.4- Contents

The program was divided into two (2) Modules, which are presented below with the questions and in Figures 2 and 3, the subject matter and methodology to be followed are illustrated and in Annexes A and B, the breakdown of the programmatic content is presented.

Module I.- The integral formation of the being from the development of the educated being to the total being.

This module will be worked on during the first four (4) weeks, guided by the following questions

S How to integrate my own domains (cognitive-conceptual, affective, physical, social, perceptual, moral and experiential) of being educated towards the formation of the Total Self?

S How do the axes (openness, reflection and integration) of human development participate in my integral formation?

s What are my competencies as a "learner" towards the integration of the primary elements of being: body, mind, emotion and spirit?

s How do I observe, accept and re-create the essence of the human being that I discover in myself? developing the following topics:

- Power of "noticing

- Domains of the educated being: cognitive-conceptual, affective, physical, perceptual, social, moral and experiential.

- Axes of human development: openness, reflection and integration

- Emotion, language and corporeality

- Effective listening

Linguistic acts: statements, declarations (judgments) and promises (requests and offers).

Module II.- The development of the experiential domain as a path to spiritual growth.

This module will be worked on during the last four (4) weeks, guided by the following questions

s How to quiet the mind?

s How to deepen the power of now?

s What can we do to expand our consciousness and recognize our essence?

s How to flow with the external world from inner wisdom?

The themes were:

- The experiential domain
- Spirituality versus religiosity
- The power of now
- Intra and interpersonal intelligence
- Breathing, visualization, relaxation.
- Observation of the mind.
- Types of meditations

The conception of the learning guide is supported by the following considerations:

The structure must guarantee the progression and accumulation of experiences and the connections between theory and praxis. Thus, the following structure is adopted:

a) Reading and personal reflection;

b) Self-observation and self-help;

c) Recording of specific exercises;

d) Reflect to transcend

The proposal of activities for each part will revolve around human development criteria: the power of *"noticing"* in order to *"take charge of..."*, the connections between theory and lived experience, the relationship between thought and action.

The different parts are proposed based on the experiential as the axis of spirituality.

The incorporation of additional procedures proposed in the curriculum of the Master's Degree in Robinsonian Education, such as *face-to-face meetings: formation of unattended groups, cooperating teachers, discussion forums and portfolio* converge towards the development of an attitude of self-management, reflective and integrative learning where the individual encounter with the discovery of frequent behavior and levels of group interaction will make you identify what limits and enhances it, in order to design actions to overcome weaknesses and expand the strengths (UNESR, Master in Robinsonian Education, 2008).

Based on the theoretical considerations of the value of self-observation, observation of the mind and meditation, the activities are proposed following the structure of learning guides, revolving around the educational thesis of the "total being". The development of the total being leads to happiness by having *the experiential* as the integrating axis of its traits, via spirituality. Criteria for analyzing the behavior of the participants as integral professionals, such as: detachment, autonomy, authenticity, fluidity, responsibility, expansion, guide the suggested activities. They are based on the conception of the total being:

> The total being is the one who has managed to develop all his capacities in an exceptional way and uses them fully in his daily life (...) happy to assume the full responsibility of his creative freedom in the search for satisfactory answers to the questions of his existence (Legendre, 1995, p.185).

Practices of self-observation and observation of the mind are carried out through exercises that are assigned to the participant, with the purpose of training his capacity to "notice" the results of the actions he performs and the changes he can incorporate in the relationship between language, emotions, body and expansion of consciousness.

Among the indicators for the process of self-observation and observation of the mind, the following are derived:

- Identify the relationship between body signs (posture, gaze, gestures, tone of voice) with emotions and judgments.
- Recognize that we are not the voice we "carry" in our heads.
- Recognize if you complain a lot or deny others
- The frequency with which you feel you are right, while others are wrong.
- The frequency with which you identify some type of attachment
- The frequency of finding fault with others or criticizing and complaining about them
- Identify frequently reactive behavior
- Recognize opinions, views and judgments as thought forms that have appropriated in you the sense of "I".

- Identify that everything you resent or reject in someone else is also in you IS A PROJECTION.

- Recognize that everything you fight against becomes stronger
- The practice of yoga as a discipline

Figure 1: Module I: The Integral Formation of the Self from the Development of the Educated Self to the Total Self.

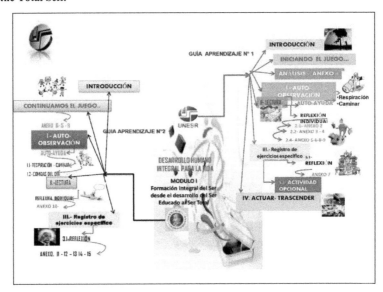

Source: Data taken from the DHIPV course syllabus. Module I. Designed by Tovar and Puertas

Figure 2: Module II: Developing the Experiential Domain of the Educated Self as a Pathway to Spiritual Growth

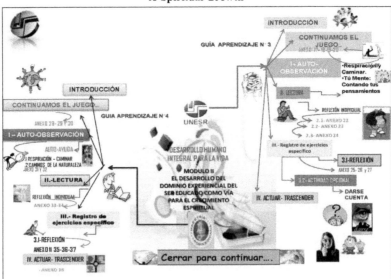

Source: Data taken from the DHIPV course syllabus. Module II Designed by Tovar and Puertas

Both modules promote the development of "knowing how to know", "knowing how to do" from "knowing how to be" and "knowing how to live together", "knowing how to create" to "knowing how to transcend". It is fundamentally directed towards personal transformation and the development of forms of self-knowledge that will allow you to recognize your strengths and areas for improvement in order to generate changes in yourself and in your environment.

It comprises a series of activities based on an updated theoretical support combined with a set of experiences, in which the enjoyment, the interactive dialogue and the experiences of the participants allow the creative contribution of all and the transfer of learning to the personal and professional environment.

2.3.5- Activities

These activities were developed as follows

Training of DHIPV course facilitators.

Two meetings or workshops were offered, attended by all eight (8) teachers of the course, who were trained on March 13 and 14, 2009 in an introductory workshop called "Towards the implementation of a new educational paradigm based on Human Development" facilitated by Dr. Beatriz Ceballos and supported by Prof. Nersa Colmenares and coordinated by Maritza Puertas. The workshop lasted two days: 12 hours face-to-face and 8 hours online. The program of the workshop is presented in Annex C, and a second workshop in the first week of April, where tools for the implementation of the DHIPV course program were proposed (see Annex D).

Face-to-face meetings at the beginning and end of the course: During the program, two (02) meetings were held, at the beginning of the course (April, 2009) (see Annex E) and at the end of the course (July, 2009) (see Annex F), with a duration of one day each meeting, with the objective of bringing the participants closer to the contents to be studied in depth, in a theoretical, practical and experiential manner. In the first one, the theoretical and methodological criteria for the development of the learning guides are provided. The second is offered as a space for reflection that contributes to broaden the evaluation of the process of self-knowledge and individual transformation.

Formation of working groups: During the first meeting, working groups of five to eight participants were formed with the objective of developing teamwork competencies by discussing and sharing the support material (readings, DVD videos, audiocassettes and films) and the activities designed, mainly on-line. In the formation of the Study Groups, special emphasis will be placed on diversity in favor of inclusion, respect and complementarity as a way towards the integral development of each participant.

Cooperating Teachers: Each region is assigned several teachers, who have an accompanying figure, who models, mediates and reinforces the contents that are being acquired (See Table 2).

Discussion forums: four (4) forums were developed during the development of the four (4) learning guides in order to exchange experiences and ideas of the participants' learning process.

Readings and written assignments: cutting-edge readings and readings from other organizational contexts applicable to the educational environment are contemplated. The results of these readings, their reflections, synthesis and, above all, the connections and applications to their particular and teaching experience are reported in the portfolio by each participant following the indications contained in the two Modules with their four (4) Learning Guides and reported in the portfolio and online. Table 4 below summarizes the readings assigned in the DHIPV course, which were listed as on-line attachments.

Table 4: Distribution of assignments in Modules I and II and their respective learning guides in the Integral Human Development for Life course.

READINGS, FILM AND VIDEOS	GUIDE I	GUIDE II
MODULE I	1 movie and 6 readings	10 readings
MODULE II	11 readings	2 CDs; 6 readings and a video
TOTAL	1 movie and 17 readings	2 CDs; 16 readings and a video

Source: DHIPV course syllabus for Module I and II. Own elaboration.

Self-observation and body work practices: These practices are carried out through exercises assigned to the participant, with the purpose of training his/her capacity to "notice" the results of the actions he/she performs and the changes he/she can incorporate in his/her language, *emotions, body and expansion of consciousness.*

Table 5 below summarizes the observation and body work practices assigned in the DHIPV course, which were developed in the network.

Table 5: Distribution of self-observation and body work assignments in Modules I and II and their respective learning guides in the Integral Human Development for Life course.

SELF-OBSERVATION AND BODY WORK	GUIDE I	GUIDE II
MODULE I	1.-Observe your breathing and quiet your mind. 2.- Observe your walk	1.-Observe your breathing and your walk 2.- Observe yourself in some of the meals of the day.
MODULE II	1.-Watch your breathing and walk 2.- Observe your mind	1.-Observe your breathing and your walk 2.- Learning the ways of nature

Source: Data taken from the DHIPV course syllabus of Module I and II. Own elaboration

Portfolio: organization of all the material used in the learning process, This work was posted on the network. This medium allowed us:

Provide comprehensive **information** on learning

• Admits the use of **continuous assessment** for the learning process.

• It has a **cooperative character**, involving facilitators, participants, organization and development of the task.

• When developing this strategy, the participant **projects the diversity of learning** that he/she has internalized. In this model, positive learning, problem situations, and strategies used in the execution of tasks are detected.

• **Results** can be **shared** with other colleagues and teachers.

• It promotes the **autonomy** of the participant and reflective critical thinking that on the one hand ensures the minimum learning and on the other hand, that which each one wishes to acquire and deepen.

• Provides the participant with good **cognitive and social habits.**

• It has a great **motivating and stimulating** component for the participants as it is a continuous work where the efforts and results achieved are quickly verified.

• It has from the beginning the criteria by which the participants will be evaluated.

• The portfolio is a **customized and creative product**, so no two are alike.

Central criterion of the evaluation: authenticity and openness in the answers. These will be shown in a clear, sincere and fluent way. Due to the experiential nature of the proposed learning guides, there is no good or bad answer, since there is no good or bad experience. The experience simply "is". What each participant can show is his or her capacity for *openness, reflection and integration* in connection with his or her experiences. And a guide to the process of self-evaluation and co-evaluation in the process of formation and transformation of the participant is presented (See appendix G and H).

2.4. - Theoretical Foundation

The proposal of this course is based on the dimensions of Education: *knowledge, experiences and values*. The knowledge selected in this case are those referring to four cardinal points such as: *Knowing How to Be, Knowing How to Live Together, Knowing How to Create and Knowing How to Transcend.*

The operationalization of these four points would help the facilitator learn to know how to transcend, "to learn to be, to situate oneself and to become", passing through several stages: Primary Being, Educated Being, Educated Being and Total Being (Legendre, 1995).

At the intersection of the Educated Self and the Total Self the educated person is "one who experiences the pleasure of promoting a variety of projects for herself and in which diverse paths contribute to increase her understanding and sensitivity to the world" (Peters, 1972, cited by Legendre, 1983).

For Legandre, 1995: p. 203) "the educated being is a being of conscious and voluntary development. The evolution of his whole being towards the actualization of his potentialities is the philosophy and the priority meaning of his life".

The educated being arises from the integral and harmonious development of the conceptual, affective, experiential, physical, moral, perceptual and social domains, as well as from the human development axes: openness, reflection and integration (Legendre, 1995, cited by Ceballos, 2003, p.200). As well as the axes of human development: *openness, reflection and integration* (Legendre, 1995, cited by Ceballos, 2003, p.200).

In this same order and direction, Ceballos (2008) ratifies and shares Legendre's (1995) approach when he affirms that the integral development of the educated being leads firstly to the formation of the total being with *Love, Autonomy and Authenticity* as fundamental pillars. Secondly, towards *Freedom, Truth and Creativity*. All this connected with Spirituality as a fundamental dimension of the human being.

The Total Being is "a being of culture in its most global and complete meaning", and that "the utopia is to become a Total Being" concludes Legendre (1995: p 204). The set of domains (*cognitive, affective, physical, moral, perceptual, social and experiential*) evolves to the development of the being, turning it into an Educated Being that according to Legendre (1993) and Ceballos (2003) is "a being in conscious and voluntary development. The evolution of his whole being towards the actualization of his potentialities is the philosophy and the priority meaning of his life in order to approach the features of the Total Being" (p. 4).

- *The Cognitive and conceptual (*Intellectual brain) develops to autonomy: It is the acquisition of knowledge, skills and abilities that allow the use of this knowledge.

- *The Physical* develops to authenticity: It encompasses sensory stimulation, mental and emotional disposition from corporeality (self-image and self-concept).

- *o Affective* (heart-emotions, affective-emotional) develops into love: It comprises empathy, feelings, interests, attitudes, values, sensitivity and adaptability.

- *The Social* develops towards freedom, the cooperative, solidary of transcendent citizen service. It includes the development of the perception of others, the interpretation of their intentions, their feelings, their role and situation in society, that is to say, to go beyond oneself.

- interpretation of their intentions, their feelings, their role and situation in society, that is to say, to go beyond oneself.

- *The Ethical-Moral* develops towards the search for the truth of the self. It encompasses the development of an action according to a personal thinking, integrated and respectful of others, knowledge, understanding and critical appreciation of actions and their consequences for the environment, as well as for the perception of the rules and fundamental principles.

- *The Perceptual* develops towards the stimulation of creativity.

- *The experiential* develops into spirituality (Legendre, 1993; 1999, Ceballos, 2003).

The Legendre Model or network of SER TITAL characteristics is shown in Figure 3.

Figure 3: Model for the Integral Formation of the Self from the Development of the Educated Self to the Total Self: Network of the characteristics of the TOTAL BEING

Source: Legendre, 1983,1993;1995, 1999 Entre l'angoisse et le reve. Montreal: Guérin.

Within the framework of sensitization and pedagogical accompaniment for the process of change that teachers should have and thus contribute to the transformation of education, the proposal of Ceballos (2006), on transformational learning and being educated, is considered important.

As for Transformational Learning, it is framed in a process that encompasses the following aspects:

4- *Observe* (Perceive and dialogue).

4- *Reflect* (Criticize, Understand, accept, appreciate, realize, moral conscience).

4- *Design* (build, be creative, innovative, detect needs).

4- *Redesign* (resizing of needs, goals and objectives).

4- *Acting* (Ethical when the projects are realized transcends to the society citizenship).

Under these premises, the reflective act is encouraged as the way for subjectivation, transformational learning and its effects on the pedagogical task.

In relation to the educated being, it arises "...from the integral and harmonious development of the cognitive-conceptual, affective, experiential, physical, moral, perceptual and social domains, as well as from the axes of human development: openness, reflection and integration" (p. 88); these axes of development correspond to three categories "...openness with listening; reflection with questioning and integration with synthesis" (p.89).

These axes of development are basic for the process of sensitization of teachers, since they allow and make possible the willingness to face changes and new situations of the teaching task in the context of educational transformation. In this sense, according to Ceballos (ob.cit), the following can be affirmed:

Openness implies aspirations, knowing potentialities and limitations, it is linked to the ability to develop listening as a process of hearing, interpreting and perceiving.

Reflection is related to critical awareness, as a process of thinking about what we do and how, what we want to change or incorporate. In other words, questions that allow reflection before action in order to propose new situations. Questioning promotes the development of reflection, the results of which will depend on effective listening.

Integration, understood as the "ability to organize and incorporate data in the context of their acquisitions and experiences; coherent formation of their knowledge, skills, attitudes and values" (p. 80).

The synthesis that expresses the development of the educated being in the cognitive-conceptual (brain), affective (emotions) and physical (body).

Maturana's (1993-1999) thesis on transformation in coexistence gave us the basis to work on language as a way of living together in the flow of the recurrent coordinations of our actions and Echeverría (1996) to study the understanding of human beings that "allow them to become pioneers and leaders in their respective fields" (p. 19).

We do things with our bodies and flow in language in our daily dialogic communication interactions.

The structure of our bodies changes according to our way of flowing in language (just look at the enlargement in the size of the brain that the use of language meant for our first ancestors). Maturana (1999) states that nothing we do in language is irrelevant, because we transform ourselves in our bodies according to what we do with language, and what we do with it transforms our bodies.

Language, as a cultural trait of oral tradition, together with amorality, as a biological trait, constitute the core of the way of life preserved generation after generation, which defined us as human beings in our evolutionary history three or more million years ago.

The biology of love is the relational dynamic that originates the quality of the human in the history of our lineage. Only "love expands intelligent behavior," says Maturana (1999, p. 53). When we speak we imply, evoke or connote the biology of love.

Love is an emotion, a way of living together, a type of relational behavior in human systems. Love occurs when in our life and interaction with others, the other, no matter who or what, emerges as a legitimate other in coexistence with us. Love (loving) is the emotion that constitutes and preserves social life.

Love is the foundation that makes possible what we wish to do.

The conception of education and pedagogy adopted is of humanistic orientation, in which the integral conception of man, as a Total Being, is assumed. Keeping in mind this conception of man, education and the world implies a radical transformation of the way teachers act.

A performance that transcends the mere transmission of knowledge and enters the world of skills to do and think, and of values to decide to choose and live freely.

It is to accept education as a social process that... "encourages man to act as an agent of his own development. "encourages man to act as an agent of his own development and to achieve the fullest realization of his potentialities" (López and Martin, 2000, p.13). It implies providing the means for human development, understood as the realization of all the potentialities of each person. To this end, we consider the importance of developing a permanent attitude of reflexive empowerment, transformation, self-correction and enrichment to achieve this human development. These principles will guide the scope of this program, framed by the following purposes of education, according to Legendre:

- "Education constitutes the indispensable assistance for every human being to satisfy his desire to learn to live, to become and to situate himself."

- "Education must focus on the fundamental aspirations of the human being and on a society in irreversible evolution".

- The ideal that education proposes to every human being is transcendence. The path of the formation of the educated being."

According to this author, the process of formation of the human being is a continuum: from the primitive being, being instructed to the educated being (the center of the teacher's concern), with the aspiration of becoming a Total Being.

The educated being arises from the integral and harmonious development of the following domains: cognitive-conceptual (cognitive and metacognitive processes); affective (feelings, emotions, interests, attitudes, values, sensitivity and adaptive capacity); physical (sensory stimulation; mental and emotional disposition from the corporeality); perceptual (the senses: visual, auditory, tactile, olfactory, gustatory and social); social (development of perception of the other, interpretation of his intentions, his feelings, his role and situation in social society); moral (knowledge, understanding and critical appreciation of the other, interpretation of his intentions, his feelings, his role and situation in social society). olfactory, gustatory and social); social (development of the perception of others, the interpretation of their intentions, their feelings, their role and situation in social society); moral (knowledge, understanding and critical appreciation of actions and their consequences for the environment); experiential (ability of self-awareness, self-evaluation and projection of learning as an integral being). Ceballos, (2008).

The traits that are transvalued and developed will constitute new faces, more evolved, are responsible for a change of culture. These are gathered in the proposal of the Total Being model: Love, Autonomy, Authenticity and Creativity, Truth, Freedom, all permeated by spirituality, from the experiential as the integrating domain, which connect us with self-knowledge in consideration of the intimate relationship between the primary elements of being: body, emotion, language or mind and spirit.

As the child learns to use language, he creates with others different ways of living, given the different events in which he participates; and he becomes in his body according to the use of the language in which he grows up. As a result, as an adult, he creates the world he lives in as an expansion of the world he created as a child.

In relation to the meaning of spirituality in changing an educational culture, he states:

> Spiritual expansion is an experience of expansion of the consciousness of belonging to a wider sphere than that of the particular environment of one's own living. This larger space can be the human community to which one belongs, the vital sphere of the biosphere, the cosmos as the domain of all existence.... .it is not distinguished from reason nor is it indicated in the description, but belongs to emotion and is only connotable as an experience of unity of a wider sphere that appears as an expansion of the consciousness of being...it is different from religious experience because it is not associated to

> no doctrine....the expansion of the consciousness of belonging (the experience of unity with the whole) that spiritual experience is, broadens sensitivity, opens the vision, loosens attachment. (Maturana, 1999, p.18)

Maturana's approach (1993-1999) complements this model of the total being by considering love as the emotion that sustains the social relationship. He promotes transformation in coexistence. In this sense, he considers that the purpose of education is to guide the subject in the path of becoming human beings who respect themselves and others through the continuous generation of coexistence spaces that originate collaboration, solidarity, commitment, joy and responsible freedom. Thus, education assumes a process of transformation in coexistence in the spaces of the family or school, public spaces through networks of conversations based on love, emotion of relational behaviors through which the other emerges as a legitimate other in coexistence with oneself.

2.5.- The axes of human development and the transformational learning cycle.

The achievement of developing all the domains of the educated being towards the total being is guaranteed only when in the teaching praxis the axes of the human being are deepened: openness, reflection and integration, according to Legendre.

Educational experiences carried out in the country have validated the relevance of the application of these axes in the integral formation of the being. Their applicability and reflections on the results have led to define the scope of each axis in correspondence with three categories: openness with listening and adaptability, reflection with questioning and integration with the capacity for synthesis, all in cumulative and progressive articulation (Ceballos, 2008).

The integration of the axes of human development is assumed from the conception of the so-called transformational learning cycle: *observe/reflect-accept/appreciate-design-redesign-act.* Blesa (2000). From this model, in combination with the model of the *observer, action and results* (Maturana (1999) and Echeverría (1996).

This perspective has been applied in teacher training (UPEL-IPC) according to Ceballos (2005 and 2008) in combination with the conception of the question from transformational learning, in the search to inquire about reality, from the results to reconstruct the process and "realize" the factors and indicators that allow the integral growth of the being, and decision making to design possible actions for change.

Purposes:

- *S* To understand that education is one of the fundamental ways to achieve the transcendence of the human being: from being educated, to being educated to total being.

- *S* Contribute to the empowerment or legitimization of participants to enable and facilitate their growth as human beings who respect themselves and others, with social and ecological awareness, so that they can act responsibly and freely in the community to which they belong.

- S To create a space of reflective knowledge and action capabilities in the future Robinsonian teacher so that he/she can project this learning, from the correction of doing and not of being, through the development of the domains of the educated being and the principles of transformational learning so that he/she can contribute to its conservation and transformation in a responsible manner in coherence with the environment where he/she develops.

All this leads to the production of new knowledge, and to the collective recovery of the lived history, where man, in reconstructing the practice, identifies its elements, classifies them, orders them, makes them objective, and thus converts his life experience in permanent change and transformation, allowing to objectify the different elements that intervened in the training process, to value it and recognize the identity factors that have been maintained despite all the changes that have occurred both personally and professionally (Jara, 1994)....*they cut off our leaves and branches, they cut our trunks, but they never managed to cut our roots" (p.9)*

The systematization of experiences acquires importance in educational contexts because it enables the construction of national pedagogical theory from the teaching praxis. The interpretation and reconstruction of experiences facilitate improvements and/or educational transformations, allow knowing what progress has been made, how much and how, with the participation of all members of the educational process.

Chapter 3

III. FORMULATE A SYSTEMATIZATION PLAN

It is necessary to develop a pedagogy of the question. We are always hearing a pedagogy of the answer. Teachers answer questions that students have not asked.

Paulo Freire

3.1. - Why do we want to systematize? The definition of the systematization objective

General Objective

- Systematize the development of an experience of the training process lived in/by the participants of the Master in Robinsonian Education in the course Integral Human Development for Life (DHIPV).

Specific objectives

- Discuss the systematization process.
- Describe the facts developed in the training process of the participants within the framework of the DHIPV course.
- Reconstruct the experience to be systematized through an orderly look at the practice and the context within the framework of the DHIPV course, lived by the participants in the three nuclei (Apure, Maracay and San Juan de los Morros).
- To identify the constants, particularities and innovative elements of the systematized experiences through a five-stage proposal within the framework of the DHIPV course.
- To analyze, based on the data obtained, the achievements and difficulties encountered by the participants during the training experience in the Integral Human Development for Life course.
- To explain the process experienced by the participants, bringing to light the new knowledge gained during the experience in the DHIPV course.

3.2. - What experience do we want to systematize (delimit the object to be systematized)?

This paper will describe the training experiences lived in/by the participants of the Master's Degree in Robinsonian Education in the course Integral Human Development for Life enrolled in the 2009-I academic period in the South (Apure) and Central (Canoabo, Maracay and San Juan de los Morros) zones.

3.3. - What central aspects are we most interested in (specify a systematization axis) and what sources of information do we have and what do we need?

The integrating thematic axes are identified with two axiological theoretical approaches: *The integral formation of the being from the development of the educated being to the Total being and The development of the experiential domain as a way for spiritual growth.*

The integral formation of the being from the development of the educated being to the Total being develops guided by the following questions

- How to integrate my domains (cognitive-conceptual, affective, physical, social, perceptual, moral and experiential) of the educated self towards the formation of the total self?

- How do the axes (openness, reflection and integration) of human development participate in my integral formation?

- What are my competencies as a "learner" towards the integration of the primary elements of being: body, mind, emotion and spirit?

- How do I observe, accept and re-create the essence of the human being I discover in myself?

The contents covered in answering these questions are as follows: Power of "noticing", Domains of the educated being: cognitive-conceptual, affective, physical, perceptual, social, moral and experiential, Axes of human being development: openness, reflection and integration, Emotion, language and corporeality, Effective listening. Linguistic acts: affirmations, statements (judgments) and promises (requests and offers).

The development of experiential mastery as a path to spiritual growth is guided by these questions:

- How to quiet the mind?

- How to deepen the power of now?

- What can we do to expand our consciousness and recognize our essence?

- How to flow with the external world from inner wisdom?

The contents covered in answering these questions are as follows: The experiential domain, spirituality versus religion, The power of now, Intra and interpersonal intelligence, Breathing, Visualization, Relaxation, Observation of the mind, Types of meditations, Yoga as a discipline.

The selected procedure was based on the analysis and discussion of the bibliography and videos, work in small groups (unassisted groups), reflections and experiential exercises in order to initiate the participant in human formation as the axis of a learning process for transcendence. These activities are integrated in two learning modules organized in four learning guides where the conception and structure adopted in them allows the organization of questions based on the experiences arising from the relationship between *body, mind, emotion and spirit*, the domains of the educated being/total being and axes of human development of each participant.

3.4. - Why do we want to do this systematization?

Personal conditions:

- Interest in learning from the experience of the Integral Human Development for Life course, from their own practice, valuing it as a source of teaching and learning in the formation of teachers participating in the Master's Degree in Robinsonian Education.

- Sensitivity to let it speak for itself and for the participants who lived the experience, seeking not to influence the observation and analysis with prejudices or justifications.

Institutional conditions:

- Search for coherence for teamwork, positioning it as an opportunity for critical reflection, inter-learning and construction of shared thinking.

- Give it real priority, assigning time and resources that guarantee that it can be adequately carried out in other cohorts of the master's program.

Chapter 4

IV. RECOVERY OF THE LIVED PROCESS

"The systematization of practices" **states that systematization**
arises from the need to know ourselves, to make ourselves
known and to qualify our practices.

Luz Dary Ruiz Botero

4.1. - Reconstruct the history of the experience of the Integral Human Development for Life (DHIPV) course, sort and classify the information.

The DHIPV course is immersed in the Master in Robinsonian Education in the second (2) Component of Deepening,[2] of the three (3) proposed in the curricular structure: Component of Problematization (seen in the first semester), and Component of Consolidation (in the last two semesters).

This component is offered in the second semester, from May 6 to July 31, 2009, with a duration of eight (8) weeks of virtual activity.

In this third "time" of systematization, the aim is to make an orderly reconstruction of what happened in the experience, as it occurred, usually chronologically, according to the period delimited.

At this point it is possible to identify the significant periods, the main choices made, the changes that marked the process, the rhythm of the process and to locate the stages that followed the process of the experience.

The course information is then reconstructed, sorted and classified.

DHIPV presented in activities taking into account time and space:

4.2. - Starting level or sensitization phase

A first face-to-face meeting was held at the beginning of the course (see appendix E) (April 2009) with the objective of:

- Self-observe the relationship between emotion, body and language or mind.
- Knowledge of basic emotions: joy, love, anger, sadness and fear.
- Notion: private conversations
- Generality of effective listening (hearing, interpreting and perceiving)
- Identify that we are not thoughts. That we are pure consciousness.
- The enemies of learning
- The trials

---

[2] the convergent vision of classical education to advance in the construction of knowledge from a divergent perspective that reflects the multi- and interdisciplinary tendencies present in the complex, diverse and plural reality in which the educational process takes place. (Design of the Master's Degree in Robinsonian Education, 2008: p. 33).

- The language-emotion relationship
- The flow
- The balance between giving and receiving
- Limiting schedules
- Body-emotion relationship

4.3. - Development level or virtual phase

The activities carried out were:

1. The facilitator's forum, the virtual facilitator, the participant's news forum, the meeting point, the course library, resources and supports, the support library, and the glossaries.

2. Reading the links for the support to be received and the information from the facilitators and virtual dynamizer.

3. A week of socialization that begins with the welcome, followed by the Navigator's Compass, the forum for personal introduction to the course, the forum for introductions of the group that did not attend, until reaching the forums sharing questions and answers, and the navigator's weekly.

4. Once the thematic development, the chronogram and the evaluation plan had been analyzed, the personal presentations and those of the unattended groups called Marineras a la Mar began.

5. Socialization forums with all participants and the facilitator where they expressed their concerns and expectations related to the course.

6. The elaboration of a portfolio of modules I and II, in order to capture their experiences in the four learning guides. Corroborate the intensity and understanding of the subject matter, through readings, exercises and interpretation and analytical observation, reflective and critical thinking of each of the components proposed in the course, and thus be able to dialogue with the unattended groups, the facilitator, the writings and the self and quality of learning in each participant to build it, the learning process and creativity in its development.

4.4. Closing level or Evaluation phase

A second face-to-face closing or evaluation session was scheduled (see Annex G), at the end of the course (September 2009) with the objective of:

1. Directly share the questions and reflections that have arisen throughout the course and especially to be able to participate in their experience of silence with the facilitator and their peers. It is the process of realizing from the exploration of the present moment to act more consciously with their families, friends, colleagues and the community in general.

2. Evaluate the DHIPV course in order to take into account the recommendations in future openings of the Master in Robinsonian Education.

Chapter 5

*Man's progress was possible because reason had dared to
think against reason.*

Lakatos

V. THE BASIC REFLECTIONS: WHY DID WHAT HAPPENED HAPPEN HAPPEN?

The purpose of this chapter is to carry out an orderly and systematic process of information through the analysis, synthesis and critical interpretation of the main events that occurred throughout the experience lived in the DHIPV course, as well as to relate theory with practice in greater depth, identifying the main achievements reached through the six criteria generated, the motivations that the participants had in staying and completing the course, the reactions of the participants in the course through the answers they provided in their portfolios in the development of the two learning modules, and the grades obtained in the course.

5.1. - Performance analysis, synthesis and interpretation

A total of 442 participants enrolled in the Master's in Robinsonian Education, in the Integral Human Development for Life (DHIPV) course, cohort 2009- I, in 26 centers of the Universidad Nacional Experimental Simón Rodríguez (UNESR) distributed throughout the country. 380 of them, 86%, completed the course, which is equivalent to a high level of permanence. Of these, 380 students completed the course, 86%, a figure that is equivalent to a high level of permanence (See Annex J).

In the three nuclei under study (Apure, Maracay and San Juan de Los Morros), 70 students were enrolled (see appendix K), showing a predominant female participation, approximately two women for every man. This participation is higher in the San Juan de los Morros Nucleus (approximately 3 to 1), as shown in the following table.

Table 6: Distribution of Participants, according to Nucleus and Gender

NUCLEUS	SEX		
	Female	Male	Total
Apure	14	11	25
Maracay	13	6	19
San Juan de Los Morros	19	7	26
TOTAL	**46**	**24**	**70**

There was a high level of attendance (56 participants sent papers, that is, 80%). However, the highest non-attendance was recorded in the Apure Nucleus, which reached 40%. Of the total of 56 attendees, the vast majority passed the course (91%). The following table shows these results:

Table 7: Distribution of Participants, according to Core and Results of the Assessment

CORE	RESULTFADOS			
	Approved	Did not approve	Did not present	Total
Apure	14	1	10	25
Maracay	15	2	2	19
San Juan de Los Morros	22	2	2	26
TOTAL	**51**	**5**	**14**	**70**

Table 8: Distribution of participants, according to results of the course evaluation , by Gender

RESULTS	SEX		
	Female	Male	Total
APPROVED	36	15	51
NOT APPROVED	3	2	5
NO SHOW	7	7	14
TOTAL	**46**	**24**	**70**

An equal number of men and women dropped out (7 men and 7 women), see Table 8. When comparing the grades of those who remained in the course, it is observed that the average of women is slightly higher than that of men (4.44 vs. 4.12) and also, they are more homogeneous (standard deviation of 0.72). The figures are shown in the following table:

Table 9: Descriptive Statistics: Scores by Gender

SEX	N	Minimum	Media	Maximum	Standard Deviation

Female	39	1,00	4,44	5,00	0,72
Male	17	1,00	4,12	5,00	1,05
TOTAL	**56**	**1,00**	**4,34**	**5,00**	**0,84**

Source: Data provided by Control de Estudio. Postgraduate Dean's Office. Coordination of the Master's Degree in Robinsonian Education, 2009. Academic Period 2009-I. Caracas. Author's calculations.

However, this difference is not statistically significant, according to the results obtained in the ANOVA test (Analysis of Variance) shown below. We can assure with 95% confidence, that there is no significant difference between the grades achieved by men and women ($F = 1.757$; $p = 0.191$), figures that are observed in the following table:

Table 10: Analysis of Variance: Scores by Gender

ANOVA	Sum of Squares	Degrees of Freedom	Medium Square	F	Significance
Between groups	1,225	1	1,225	1,757	0,191
Within groups	37,658	54	0,697		
TOTAL	**38,883**	**55**			

Source: Data provided by Control de Estudio. Postgraduate Dean's Office. Coordination of the Master's Degree in Robinsonian Education, 2009. Academic Period 2009-I. Caracas. Author's calculations.

In the same way, the results of the course evaluation show very similar grades, when compared by nucleus. All the grades are higher than 4 points and only the San Juan de Los Morros Nucleus presents an average higher than the group average (4.46 vs. 4.31). It is also in this Nucleus where more homogeneous grades are observed (lowest standard deviation = 0.55). Details in the following table:

Table 11: Descriptive Statistics: Grades by Core

CORE	N	Minimum	Media	Maximum	Standard Deviation
Apure	15	1,00	4,31	4,95	0,96
Maracay	17	1,00	4,21	5,00	1,07
San Juan de Los Morros	24	3,00	4,46	5,00	0,55
TOTAL	**56**	**1,00**	**4,34**	**5,00**	**0,84**

Source: Data provided by Control de Estudio. Postgraduate Dean's Office. Coordination of the Master's Degree in Robinsonian Education, 2009. Academic Period 2009-I. Caracas. Author's calculations

The ANOVA test ratifies that these grades are statistically equal when comparing the three cores (F = 0.451; p = 0.640), as shown in the following table:

Table 12: Analysis of Variance: Scores per Core

ANOVA	Sum of Squares	Degrees of Freedom	Medium Square	F	Significance
Between groups	0,650	2	0,325	0,451	0,640
Within groups	38,233	53	0,721		
TOTAL	**38,883**	**55**			

Source: Data provided by Control de Estudio. Postgraduate Dean's Office. Coordination of the Master's Degree in Robinsonian Education, 2009. Academic Period 2009-I. Caracas. Author's calculations

5.2. - Analysis, synthesis and interpretation of the experience.

Systematizing reflection for the popular educator and sociologist Oscar Jara (1998) is characterized because it seeks to penetrate inside the dynamics of lived experiences, moving between their worlds, identifying the relationships between them, going through their different stages, locating their contradictions, tensions, marches and regressions, managing to reason these processes from their internal logic, extracting from there lessons that enrich both practice and theory.

1. For this reason, Table 13 presents the experiences and testimonies of the forty-seven (47) participants, the number of portfolios available on the UNESR network at the time (2009-I), collected in a logical linkage matrix where each experience and evidence was correlated with the achievement indicator (*"realizing"* in order to *"taking charge of"*.) identified from the review of the portfolios so creative, with so many colors, images, drawings, organization of ideas and so many opinions of being rather than doing in the realization of the activities of the two learning modules, where they expressed the levels of motivation achieved and the integrity of the elements of being: *body, mind, emotion and spirit.*

The achievement indicator **"realizing"** in order to **"take charge of"** is evidenced when the relevant behavior is identified for a change of attitude towards an integral conception of education in order to design possible actions for change in different scenarios: classroom, family or community.

Six (6) criteria emerged from this indicator for analysis:

1. *Desire to change*: when the desired situation for the transformation of an educational praxis is coherently stated.

2. *Respect for others*: when an action is formulated in attention to the needs of others.
3. *Educating for life*: when a performance is shown or criteria of an educational praxis that meets daily needs related to quality of life and ethical sense are manifested.
4. *Conscious pedagogical praxis*: when criteria and indicators of the teaching practice are manifested in relation to strategies
5. *Valuing the spiritual*: when the importance of the connection with the essence of the self is recognized.
6. *To be the protagonist of spiritual growth:* when one recognizes the ego's own actions in order to experience the essence of being: peace, joy and love.

The criteria were evaluated on a scale from 0 to 5, where 0 is the absence of the criteria; from 1 to 3 the indicator of *noticing* is observed and from 4 to 5 there is the presence of the indicator *taking charge of*. Subsequently, to sum up, the criteria were added up and the result was divided by the number of scores obtained in each experience and testimony.

From the analysis it can be observed that out of forty-seven participants, 70%, that is, 33 of them reflected in their reflections in MODULE I and II evidence of integration of their domains (cognitive, conceptual, affective, physical, perceptual, moral and experiential) embodied through the achievement indicator *"realizing"* in order to *"take charge of"*, analyzed through the six criteria (*Desire to change*, Respect for others, Educating for life, Conscious pedagogical praxis, Valuing the spiritual and Being protagonist of spiritual growth), *Respect for others, Educating for life, Conscious pedagogical praxis, Valuing the spiritual and Being a protagonist of spiritual growth),* and the rest of them 14 participants, that is, 30%, did not capture in their reflections the *respect for others, educating for life,* conscious pedagogical *praxis*, valuing the spiritual and being a protagonist of spiritual growth. It is important to highlight that 10 of the 47 participants were not able to reflect their reflections on the objectives of MODULE II in the portfolio.

These results reflect that the objective of MODULE I was achieved, referring to *the integral formation of the being from the development of the educated being to the total being"* oriented by the following questions: How to integrate my domains (cognitive-conceptual, affective, physical, social, perceptual, moral and experiential) of the educated being towards the formation of the total being?How do the axes (openness, reflection and integration) of human development participate in my integral formation; what are my competences as a "learner" towards the integration of the primary elements of being: body, mind, emotion and spirit; how do I observe, accept and re-create the essence of the human being that I discover in myself?

However, in MODULE II, in the objective of *developing the experiential domain of the educated being as a way for spiritual growth*, it was not consolidated in its totality. It was not observed in the portfolio through the answers to the questions: How to quiet the mind; How to deepen in the power of the now; What to do to expand our consciousness and recognize our essence; How to flow with the external world from the internal wisdom; How to flow with the external world from the internal wisdom, any reflection about valuing the spiritual and being protagonist of the spiritual growth.

It is important to point out that when evaluating the different portfolios, and in the last visit to the participants of the Apure, San Juan de los Morros and Maracay centers for the closing of the activity, they expressed through their opinions that Module II (activities 3 and 4) should be worked with the non-assisted group, and not individually, as follows: "it *should not be done alone because the essence of our mastery is to become a learning community based on the interaction with our non-assisted group.... Although it is true that I carried out a reflection of my personal and professional actions, it would have been more enriching to share my experiences with my non-assisted group that I appreciate so much and my family members.* "

In the same sense, of the 51 participants who satisfactorily completed the course out of the 70 enrolled, they requested that it be administered in more time, if possible in sixteen weeks and not in eight as planned, as confirmed by one student: "*that for the eight weeks the course was interesting, relevant, but very dense and short for the semester... a lot of reading material and little time to enjoy it 100%, as I would have liked to live it and savor it to the fullest.* ".

Table 13: Logical linkage matrix: Experiences, Testimonies, Achievement Indicator and Criteria of the Integral Human Development for Life course - Period II. Maracay (*), San Juan de los Morros and Apure groups.

INDICATOR	*Realize* in order to *take charge of*					
CRITERIA **EXPERIENCES AND TESTIMONIALS**	DESIRE TO CHANGE	RESPECT FOR OTHERS	EDUCATING FOR LIFE	CONSCIOUS PEDAGOGICAL PRAXIS	VALUE THE SPIRITUAL	SPIRITUAL GROWTH	TOTAL
1. "We must educate for life, the person needs to find the meaning of what he lives, what happens within him and in his environment, as teachers we cannot turn our backs on what people think, want and need.	5	5	5	5	5	0	4
Through education, human potential is developed that enables and increases people's freedom." Resignify the sense of human sensitivity, the harmony of the inner BEING, hence education will be then, interrelation between social actors, transforming knowledge into an authentic	5	5	5	5	5	0	4

existential event, allowing him not only to understand and know his environment and his being, but also to evaluate and assess his duty to be". One of the most valuable results in the study of this unit has been to get in touch with my inner self, not only in my role as a teacher, as a behavior shaper and counselor, but as a human being, the need to keep in mind the great responsibility we have in our hands leads me to make a great effort to achieve a work where quality stands out in favor of an assertive learning that will benefit a great collective".	5	5	5	5	5	0	4
We are moving towards an educational structure centered on the human aspect, which allows us to concretize knowledge, action and coexistence for the formation of a human being.	5	5	5	5	5	0	4
to be social, creative, productive and supportive and to assume education as a process of lifelong learning". This unit has given me the tools to get to know myself and my group mates, to know their concerns, and to respect their feelings and preferences.	5	5	5	5	5	0	4
6 Knowing what emotions, sensations and judgments emerge from me helped me to design some actions that brought me closer and closer to evidencing experiences that helped me to realize what happens to me as an individual, and also helped me to know and understand my work group". 7 To reflect on living with freedom, love, authenticity and respect. A light came to me and now I say my transformation is mine, it belongs to me and it is my own.	5	5	5	5	5	0	4

INDICATOR	Realize in order to take charge of						
CRITERIA	DESIRE TO CHANGE	RESPECT FOR OTHERS	EDUCATING FOR LIFE	CONSCIOUS PEDAGOGICAL PRAXIS	VALUING THE SPIRITUAL	SPIRITUAL GROWTH	TOTAL
EXPERIENCES AND TESTIMONIALS							
I want to be a total being. What peace and tranquility I feel when I let go of all the prejudices and obstacles that prevented my life from being one of ETERNAL JOY AND ABSOLUTE HAPPINESS."	5	0	5	0	5	5	3
8. "Education leads us to live and act in respect for ourselves and respect for others, allows us to operate with social awareness and behave with responsibility and freedom within a community".	5	5	4	4	4	0	4

9. "I feel very happy to have assimilated and cast aside the ego that confused my mind dragging me to the past and the future, forgetting my present, my breathing, my walk and all the happiness that comes from being alive".	3	0	3	3	3	5	3
10. "...I have my conscience set on achieving that my right to have been born and to my eternal joy belongs to me and it is not a struggle but a state of consciousness".	4	0	3	0	4	5	3
I have believed that education is something deeper than covering a pre-established content, it is the training to recognize myself in my reality, enjoying and modifying the elements, as appropriate and useful to my needs in accordance with the environment, I want to feel and be a leading actor in my training process, extending it to those who allow me to share their knowledge on a daily basis".	4	4	4	4	4	0	4
To transcend the situations with which I must interact, I must realize that there are elements that I can change, those variables of my internal part, changing my way of seeing and interpreting what I consider real, I can see the changes that I am achieving, I value my emotional and spiritual growth, but I must also identify those that even when they touch me, are beyond my ability to change, which is not equivalent to conform, but to learn to work in order to achieve the means to continue growing with them, with their existence, that is to say coexisting in harmony and constant evolution".	5	5	5	5	5	3	5
13. "I confirmed my own hypothesis of believing that being educated is more than just reading and compulsively quoting author after author, it is respecting the knowledge of others, valuing nature, enjoying each achievement and working with love in each task undertaken, making those around me feel that their achievements are valuable, so that they are encouraged to improve their own practice every day, transcending weakness and turning it into strength".	5	5	5	5	5	5	5

	INDICATOR	*Realize* in order to *take charge of*						
CRITERIA		DESIRE TO CHANGE	RESPECT FOR OTHERS	EDUCATING FOR LIFE	CONSCIOUS PEDAGOGICAL PRAXIS	VALUE THE SPIRITUAL	SPIRITUAL GROWTH	TOTAL
EXPERIENCES AND TESTIMONIALS								
14. "It was easy, I felt an immense emotion of tranquility, it was as if my mind wanted to travel or move to another place. When we are focused on something in peace, there are external factors that interrupt that inner peace and stillness."		3	0	4	0	4	4	2
15. ".is the development of the person who learns and is able to be co-creator of a desirable space of social coexistence that generates collaboration, joy and freedom. It consists in the creation of conditions that guide and support the person in his or her growth to live in self-respect and respect for the other. Formation helps people grow with the capacity to do anything and learn anything with social awareness and responsibility. This capacity is necessary to respond to the world we are building in our living. Human Formation is applied to the development of the Generic Competences necessary to undertake any profession and in any field of human action (business, social).		5	5	5	5	5	5	5
16. "imaginative games and activities enriched verbal and written information with physical movements, color, depth and positive emotions, what is spoken can often be communicated by body language, attitudes, word choice and thinly veiled expectation. Although subtle, these suggestions aided by a rich variety of learning tasks, music, movements and exercises, can create a positive state of mind and raise energy levels and attention. The desire to continue learning is based on self-confidence and personal expectations, learning to determine our values in order to have a sense of direction, for without them the course of a human being's life can be altered.		5	0	5	5	5	5	4

	DESIRE TO CHANGE	RESPECT FOR OTHERS	EDUCATING FOR LIFE	CONSCIOUS PEDAGOGICAL PRAXIS	VALUING THE SPIRITUAL	SPIRITUAL GROWTH	TOTAL
17. ".I consider that with the great amount of tools for life and the different exercises performed I am traveling the path of spirituality that leads to the integral formation of the being integrating my domains (cognitive-conceptual, affective, physical, social, perceptual, moral and experiential), leading me to reflect on the process of realizing from the exploration of the present moment to act more consciously with all my surroundings family, friends, colleagues, students and all the people who in one way or another are related to me."	5	5	5	5	5	3	5

INDICATOR							
	Realize in order to _take charge_ of						
CRITERIA **EXPERIENCES AND TESTIMONIALS**	DESIRE TO CHANGE	RESPECT FOR OTHERS	EDUCATING FOR LIFE	CONSCIOUS PEDAGOGICAL PRAXIS	VALUING THE SPIRITUAL	SPIRITUAL GROWTH	TOTAL
18. "...the review of the material and the exercises were carried out collectively, that is, with the dialogic participation of the members of the unassisted group Brújula Social, each one carrying out his exercise individually, relying on empirical postures, coexistence from the human, cooperative, loving and democratic work to reach a common goal. The limitations for the capture of information and consolidation of meaningful learning is an adventure where we have to get rid of all those negative agents (fear) that influence so that what is proposed, what is planned, is not achieved".	5	5	5	5	5	5	5
19. "Education is life for personal growth, where self-respect must prevail. Freedom and responsibility are values that guide us along the path of the truth of self-concept and self-acceptance in order to achieve our goals, taking education as the axis that makes possible the intellectual space of operational and rational coexistence. ...Hence the creativity, the freedom to choose what one wants to do. Values must prevail so that there is harmony, respect for each other. That is life. It is to live it intensely from where your conscience dictates it."	5	5	5	5	5	5	5

20. "Here again, cultivating values of love towards my community by meeting myself, to then understand my neighbor, to be able to help them in this daily sharing of development of spiritual self-mastery of experience through this journey through life, maintaining a guiding thread of self-observation by reaching a sharing of language, corporeality and emotions in connection with the spiritual, to make contact with the exercises indicated in a full way. I continue in a widened way... "Absolute freedom is closer than your next breath" and thus find more and more the awareness of my nature as a total being."	5	5	5	5	5	5	5
In the workshop 11 Poetics of Living: Discipline, which I conducted with the participants of the "Language and Communication" course, I was able to appreciate that love is the driving force capable of impelling the actions of human beings towards the achievement of the common good, without any need to apply manipulative, coercive strategies that force and oblige people to simulate the fulfillment of their duties under the pressure of those who feel they have the power to govern, to direct the actions of others. There is no greater discipline than that which is established under the influence of love, with full awareness of the benefits it generates individually and socially, never under the sign of fear and abuse of authority. I am convinced that love.							
	5	5	5	5	5	5	5

INDICATOR	*Realize* in order to *take charge of*						
CRITERIA EXPERIENCES AND TESTIMONIALS	DESIRE TO CHANGE	RESPECT FOR OTHERS	EDUCATING FOR LIFE	CONSCIOUS PEDAGOGICAL PRAXIS	VALUE THE SPIRITUAL	SPIRITUAL GROWTH	TOTAL
and awareness can generate added value, because: It increases the participant's self-esteem (self-esteem) * It allows everyone to feel important. "It encourages the development of collaborative learning." 22. "I have already put into practice several activities that you have given me as homework to my participants of the UNESR, see the movie the dead poets' society, we analyzed it together, the poem of the bad girl, the power of noticing, the enemies of learning, among others.... Thank you teacher as I have read and learned. Above all fill me with patience. ... one experiences that thoughts, feelings, perceptions and actions continue: they were always caused by the action and interaction of the fundamental forces of nature. But now there is no more complication with the ego, no more any thought that "I am thinking, feeling, perceiving, acting." Thank you for the experience							
	5	5	5	5	5	5	5

23. "It is important to emphasize that human beings are not and will not be prepared to endure being offended, ignored and displaced from the social context in which they develop. It is essential to feel accepted, respected and valued as he/she is...in this way it will be easier to form and insert him/herself into the social environment, since disqualifications or denials of the human being significantly detract from the meaning of life and doing for ....the sake of ....life. On the contrary, acceptance restores the meaning of life and being...". "I feel very well with a great desire to continue learning and already putting into practice what I have learned so far. The experience has been very rewarding and fruitful from all areas."	5	5	5	5	5	5	5
24. "As teachers we must assume the commitment to educate for life, to learn to see the hearts of our students without pretending that they become automatons capable of repeating content empty of meaning, but rather that they become total beings with autonomy, creativity, dreams and goals to achieve. In this sense, substantial changes must be made in our educational model, in order to overcome the traditionalist, vertical, punitive dogmas of a closed school and replace them with schools for life, which value human beings in all their facets, which provide them with tools to find themselves, which favor effective communication, which enhance their abilities to live and learn.	5	5	5	5	5	5	5
to transcend... to educate for life is to open our hearts and extend a hand to hope and love in order to forge a more humane, supportive and happy world in communion with our fellow men". ..." I would like to end by congratulating professors Maritza and Beatriz for including this							

INDICATOR	*Realize* in order to *take charge of*						
CRITERIA EXPERIENCES AND TESTIMONIALS	DESIRE TO CHANGE	RESPECT FOR OTHERS	EDUCATING FOR LIFE	CONSCIOUS PEDAGOGICAL PRAXIS	VALUING THE SPIRITUAL	SPIRITUAL GROWTH	TOTAL
a subject that has given us wonderful tools to live, to love, to feel, to be in love, in solidarity and in the hope of the total being in fullness of life and happiness". To understand the meaning of each of the dimensions of human development (openness, reflection and integration), in the conceptual, affective, physical, perceptual, social, moral and experiential domains applicable to the different functions that we must perform (personally and professionally), from the processes of self-knowledge, self-esteem, self-direction and self-efficacy in order to achieve the personal well-being that we need. To reach the competences that will allow us to understand education as the expeditious way for the transformation of the human being from the educated being to the educated being in order to reach the total being. For this, it is necessary to distinguish those enemies of learning that may be present in us, but also to generate those enemies that may be present in us, but also to generate those enemies that may be present in us, but also those enemies that may be present	5	5	5	5	5	5	5

open spaces that propitiate the formation of a teacher as an integral being. To create a space of reflective knowledge and action capabilities that as a teacher allows me to project from doing, through the development of the domains of the educated being and the principles of transformational learning. To propitiate spaces for the applicability of the knowledge learned and/or strengthened in the teaching and personal practice that generate a transformational learning in our students and children, conceiving actions that induce them to "realize" who they are and what they want from the search and the inquiry of reality, from the results to reconstruct the process that allow them the integral growth of the being".							
26. "The enriched knowledge that I have acquired during the learning process has been the starting point to understand and do things better, with solid bases of knowledge, that is to say, to do-feel and to know. Humility, spirituality, responsibility, emotions and actions are even more clear and rooted as an integral being. Going through the readings, exercises and reflections of the course, has enriched me and	5	5	5	5	5	5	5
reaffirmed my values and knowledge even more. Education gives us the opportunity to bring out the best in us, and is the way to compensate for negativities. Acting on the law of love is							

INDICATOR	***Realize*** **in order to** ***take charge of***						
CRITERIA **EXPERIENCES AND TESTIMONIALS**	DESIRE TO CHANGE	RESPECT FOR OTHERS	EDUCATING FOR LIFE	CONSCIOUS PEDAGOGICAL PRAXIS	VALUE THE SPIRITUAL	SPIRITUAL GROWTH	TOTAL
to remain attentive to the figures or weaknesses in relationships in order to reestablish bonds by healing them through understanding, forgiveness and concrete action of reparation. It is necessary to act as a conciliator through respect and understanding, seeking in every situation of confrontation the coincidences to move forward for the benefit of harmony."							

EXPERIENCES AND TESTIMONIALS	DESIRE TO CHANGE	RESPECT FOR OTHERS	EDUCATING FOR LIFE	CONSCIOUS PEDAGOGICAL PRAXIS	VALUING THE SPIRITUAL	SPIRITUAL GROWTH	TOTAL
27. .. I want to tell you that it has been a real honor to have had you as a facilitator, although you squeezed our neurons and demanded time on ourselves, I really thank you from my heart, because I did something that I have not done for a long time, expressed in a phrase of someone "Stop the world, I want to get off". I have to tell you here, as I did in the activities, that the activities of Unit I really stressed me out and I even felt unmotivated, making judgments such as: "This does not meet my expectations of what I thought of the course" and "I am exploiting my ideas by doing an essay or the three pages", but I admit that Unit II fascinated me, I never stopped reading and I loved to repeat the activities over and over again. It fulfilled all and even more the expectations I expected from the course...I never investigated about all the techniques they had to be aware of my present. Now when I am startled by some thought from the past or some thought outside of my reality, I say to myself:... "I am not focused on my present, out of thought, this time no longer belongs to you, it is mine alone". "A thousand thanks to the universe and to the universal cosmic energy for allowing me to be in your course and with you! Thank you for existing and being among us! ON NAMASTE!.Thank you for everything you gave us! "	5	5	5	5	5	5	5
28. .. "I went through the different contents of the assignments, and I present this reflection on the basis of what education means to me.... ... to take hold of tools that allow us to expand our multipurpose capabilities in order to perform effectively and efficiently during the exercise of the teaching function, and this exercise, in my humble opinion should be directed to secular education, since I think it is up to us as teachers to encourage students to collectively build meaningful learning, based on values and principles, corresponding to the family the right and responsibility for the religious education of their children according to their convictions and in accordance with the freedom of religion and worship provided by the constitution. The objectives proposed by the facilitators are precious because they invite us to prepare ourselves as integral human beings, and thus contribute to the formation of each and every one of our children.	5	5	5	5	5	5	5
INDICATOR	*Realize* in order to *take charge of*						
CRITERIA	DESIRE TO CHANGE	RESPECT FOR OTHERS	EDUCATING FOR LIFE	CONSCIOUS PEDAGOGICAL PRAXIS	VALUING THE SPIRITUAL	SPIRITUAL GROWTH	TOTAL

I am sure that this is a meaningful construction that allows liberation and transformation that constitutes the path to freedom, happiness, respect for the other, the development of our nation and respect for this precious, but mistreated planet where we are neighbors. Although, I insist, it is so beautiful the invitation, but without the pressure that implied to comply with a schedule. However, in the future activities that I will deploy with the guidance of the light that radiates Maritza Puertas, I know that I will be able to take the hands of "Imagination", "Joy", "Enthusiasm", "Wisdom" to realize what happens inside me and recreate a being that as a teacher I can lead with "Innocence" and "Diaphanousness".							
29. "Fulfill the activities entrusted to me with more effort within the established time. One of the things I want to be honest about is the realization that as time goes by, not everything is as I thought it would be and that maturity makes us more mature. leads to constant reflection on what was presumed to be true".	4	0	4	0	0	3	2
I believe that the axes of openness, reflection and integration can be applied as long as there is full disposition to desire and work towards substantial changes in our being. This is applicable in an integral way in all the circumstances of life: in the bosom of our family, in our work, with our neighbors... How? By exercising an authentic openness to accept others. Applying effective listening, valuing all that we can learn from them. Reflection arises when we question ourselves, ask questions and critically analyze the situations that arise, while integration arises when what we have experienced becomes part of our repertoire of knowledge, of that wonderful baggage that makes a difference in our behavior and enlightens us.	5	5	5	5	5	5	5
When we experience universal love, we reach a deep sense of fulfillment, joy and inner peace that is unmatched. Thus, we walk along paths of freedom, being able to give free rein to our feelings, we become creative and vigorous, we permeate limiting barriers, allowing us to make the great leap from the micro to the macro, from the concrete to the abstract, from the profane to the sacred, in that eternal and sublime aspiration to reach transcendence. We cannot lose the objective of having been born human."							

INDICATOR	*Realize* in order to *take charge of*						
CRITERIA	DESIRE TO CHANGE	RESPECT FOR OTHERS	EDUCATING FOR LIFE	CONSCIOUS PEDAGOGICAL PRAXIS	VALUE THE SPIRITUAL	SPIRITUAL GROWTH	TOTAL
EXPERIENCES AND TESTIMONIALS							
31. "I realize that experiential development requires not only real involvement in real life, but also the very openness, reflection and integration of the data that has come out of my life and inner peace. When as educated beings we perceive our	4	0	4	0	4	4	3

dysfunctions, which hinder the cycles of Opening Reflection Integration, so that we take time to clean these resources of suffering and frustration that compromise my evolution...".							
32. " Si.... with a lot of strength, will and desire to continue learning in order to be better every day with the world around me...! WE CONTINUE THE GAME... I feel very well and I realize that all the activities I have done up to this moment, all the readings have left in me a lot of knowledge...experiences...they have really been very interesting and gratifying...-Understand the meaning of each of the dimensions of human development (openness, reflection and integration), in the conceptual, affective, physical, perceptual, social, moral and experiential domains applicable to the different functions that we must perform (personally and professionally), from the processes of self-knowledge, self-esteem, self-direction and self-efficacy in order to achieve the personal well-being that we need".	4	0	4	4	4	4	4
33. It is said: "Never underestimate the power of smiling, of being happy", from the depths of my soul I welcome you to this learning community, where I will be sharing with you my emotions and sensations, in relation to this series of activities that I have developed in this course ... for Life, ...I have acquired new knowledge, and I have been able to to find myself. In this way, this invitation has as its purpose the orientation towards the observation of the power of transformation that has the being of "realizing" the relevant conditions of our existence. I hope you enjoy this journey for your personal and professional life. Thank you for being as you are..."	5	0	5	4	4	5	4
34. "It is very important that we have this type of reflections, because through this we realize if we really have the necessary knowledge to develop our educational work, even if we do not have the necessary knowledge to develop our educational work. this also allows us to see what our mistakes are, accept them and above all correct them."	5	0	5	5	5	0	3
	3	0	4	0	0	0	1
35. "all the readings give us tools that help me redesign many aspects of my life and make the most of every moment that I have had. wasted."							

INDICATOR	*Realize* in order to *take charge of*						
CRITERIA **EXPERIENCES AND TESTIMONIALS**	DESIRE TO CHANGE	RESPECT FOR OTHERS	EDUCATING FOR LIFE	CONSCIOUS PEDAGOGICAL PRAXIS	VALUE THE SPIRITUAL	SPIRITUAL GROWTH	TOTAL
36. "To conclude this beautiful virtual meeting, it is important to highlight the teaching that this course intends to undertake, in those people who do not accept the changes.	3	3	3	3	4	3	3
who were able to spread it to look for changes and to feel that each person immersed in this mastery can achieve a path of peace? Thank you very much, it was necessary".							
37. "Reading allowed me to evoke, by way of example, some events of my life and to become aware - once again - that in reality, the my career has been on the rise, and many problems I have faced have allowed me to grow internally and externally".	4	0	3	4	4	4	3

38. "immerses us in a deep reflection that impels us to review the performance of our life, where we experience different emotions and sensations. Seen in this way, life is a learning process where we are supposed to learn a lesson, we have the sensation that we reach a world of atonement where through the crucible of the experience we transmute faults, errors, defects and vices among others. However, it happens so fast that we often seem like tourists whose heritage is circumscribed to a learned culture plagued with taboos and dogmas, forming the reflection of our mental structure".	3	0	3	0	3	3	2
The axes of human development - openness, reflection and integration - can be exercised daily in our work as teachers by keeping our minds attentive to what our students, children and co-workers are telling us. If we are willing to listen and reflect, they will surely be moments of truth that will give us opportunities to improve our work as well as our lives. The synthesis will help us in a dialectic process to improve our knowledge by integrating over the years our knowledge into our work and our lives.							
know. Surely the home with my daughters would be my first implementation to then continue in the classroom and then make it a normal and widespread practice throughout my life. To continue discovering my self, to practice some kind of meditation, to search for the truth, for God, to continue developing my human side, to study, to learn, I promise to love, to educate, to teach, to my daughters, my wife, and to my family. I promise to love and serve my neighbor. I promise to love in my work as a teacher."	5	5	5	5	5	5	5

INDICATOR	Realize in order to take charge of						
CRITERIA	DESIRE TO CHANGE	RESPECT FOR OTHERS	EDUCATING FOR LIFE	CONSCIOUS PEDAGOGICAL PRAXIS	VALUING THE SPIRITUAL	SPIRITUAL GROWTH	TOTAL
EXPERIENCES AND TESTIMONIALS							
40. "The learning in the course was: Incorporate the Love element in teaching practices. To establish strategies that develop living and doing. To diminish the enemies of learning. To develop all the domains to the fullest. To know oneself as a person, professional and human being. The formation of teacher-researcher as an "educated being" corresponds to a conception of education for life, where the educational action is reflected in the proposal of a pedagogical intervention that guarantees, with its objectives, contents and strategies, the integral development of the being through transformational learning. To develop this intentionality requires starting from education with an interdisciplinary perspective that guarantees the apprehension of the social domain in relation to other domains of the educated being, especially the cognitive, affective and experiential domain, as well as the development of the axes of the human being and its fundamental categories. To plan teaching strategies where situations of sharing, learning, cooperating, being and doing are manifested (put into practice from today). To generate in my teaching practices spaces of coexistence and learning that allow the development of love (From today). To begin to generate myself as that Integral Total Being (gradually). To take advantage of time in some aspects, (starting today). Not to be afraid of things, they must be understood and taken care of (gradually)".	5	5	5	5	5	5	5

	DESIRE TO CHANGE	RESPECT FOR OTHERS	EDUCATING FOR LIFE	CONSCIOUS PEDAGOGICAL PRAXIS	VALUE THE SPIRITUAL	SPIRITUAL GROWTH	TOTAL
41. In my teaching practice, to be more concerned with quality rather than quantity, seeking above all the expansion of total being. In the family environment, to change from the axis of having to the axis of knowing in the heart of my existence and to feel more satisfied with it. In the community that surrounds me, to play down the importance of the spirit of competition to surpass others, to beat them, but rather to seek to become fully the same, realizing that excellence is possible in everyone".	5	5	5	5	5	3	5
Very interesting, appropriate and timely development of the content of the course (DHIPV). It is well seen that the maximum interest that this Master's Degree wants to achieve is precisely the opening of a learning space that contributes to the interest that all human beings have in learning to be, to become and to situate ourselves, that is why this course has its essence in the activation of the experiential domain, based on self-observation and expansion of the inner world, in order to integrate human formation in the different areas or domains: family, school, university and community.... Let us be aware that this course will be useful to achieve the human development required in our teaching work, and that we will also achieve the integral formation required from the educated being to the total being".	5	5	5	5	5	5	5

INDICATOR	Realize in order to take charge of						
CRITERIA **EXPERIENCES AND TESTIMONIALS**	DESIRE TO CHANGE	RESPECT FOR OTHERS	EDUCATING FOR LIFE	CONSCIOUS PEDAGOGICAL PRAXIS	VALUE THE SPIRITUAL	SPIRITUAL GROWTH	TOTAL
To become aware of my actions, to plan my activities, to share more with my family and to observe myself every day.	5	4	3	4	3	3	4
44. "To strengthen myself in knowledge and give the best of myself to the students, family and environment and spiritually to myself. To understand the initiative of the students and their aspirations".	5	4	0	0	3	2	2
45. "I HAVE COME OUT OF THE MENTAL DARKNESS The moment came to my consciousness when I realized that my life had passed between the past, remembering what could have been and was not, maybe if I had done it this way it would be different, which brought to my life an imbalance that did not allow me to enjoy my present. The same thing happened with the future as well, like trying to obtain and acquire material goods to enjoy them in the future, well I have managed through this course to concentrate my consciousness in the now. With the exercises of self-observation: feeling my breathing, the way I walk, the way I eat, being open to leave aside the enemies of learning, judgments, having private conversations with myself that made me reflect that in life you have to live with freedom, love, authenticity and respect..."	5	0	4	0	5	5	3

46. " Hello everyone! Doing a little mental exercise I find today that doing a little meditation while sleeping my baby in my arms, dropping our weight in a hammock llanera, I realize that little by little I am dominating my thoughts, thoughts that now I understand sometimes became hidden fears. Well, the way to optimize the results is precisely by doing the Ishayas exercises and techniques, for this, what I do is to be relaxed and turn my gaze inward, in that absolute darkness of my being, maintaining total stillness, so that when I am approached by those thoughts, I immediately recognize the emotion behind that fear, and therefore the cause or reason for that emotion. In such a way, I accept the emotion and recognize it as such, but I eliminate the thought by placing another thought or memory that invades my being with happiness. These actions have been helpful to me lately and make me recognize in myself the unlimited human being that I am, in perfect harmony with the universe. I hope you find my experience helpful. Best regards and see you next time!	5	0	5	0	5	5	3

INDICATOR	Realize in order to take charge of						
CRITERIA **EXPERIENCES AND TESTIMONIALS**	DESIRE TO CHANGE	RESPECT FOR OTHERS	EDUCATING FOR LIFE	CONSCIOUS PEDAGOGICAL PRAXIS	VALUE THE SPIRITUAL	SPIRITUAL GROWTH	TOTAL
47. With frankness I can tell you that my form of behavior and life from the spiritual to the performance with respect to the exercise and integral growth of knowledge, have elevated in my being a greater commitment of security in the decisions that concern me to execute. Practicing daily the different forms of meditation: mind, thought and conscience; has been very productive because I look for my conscience to be transparent, moving away the thoughts that hinder my actions. In the same way I feel the satisfaction of serving as a facilitator to my participants and environment that in one way or another I have facilitated my learning and today they put it into practice with great interest.	5	5	5	5	5	5	5

Source: Information provided by the participants in the portfolio of the Nuclei: Apure, Maracay and San Juan de los Morros Academic Period 2009-I.

Chapter 6

VI.   THE ARRIVAL POINTS

If you change with every experience you make,"
Master Muto once asked one of his disciples, "what is
it in you that remains unchanged?
-- The way to constantly change responded."

Michael Ende

Thus, with the experience lived in the DHIPV course, with the testimonies and experiences of a group of participants from the Nuclei of Apure, Maracay and San Juan de los Morros, I drew up these conclusions and recommendations for the communication of the lessons learned and the projections that can be transferred from the aforementioned work.

I ventured to systematize and present this experience, with humility, but also with the conviction of the validity of the practice in its personal and professional dimension, as an expression of its historical construction and in order to allow us to direct our training action to make it transformative, both of the reality that surrounds us, as well as of ourselves as human beings.

6.1. Formulate conclusions and recommendations

The systematization of the experience we have carried out was a need felt by the researcher, coordinator and at the same time one of the eight facilitators of the DHIPV course, of the Master's Degree in Robinsonian Education. We can affirm that this need is based on the very nature of the human being, who demands to live in an environment that allows and provides a full life, for happiness, love, peace, not only personally, but also collectively, and to be able to crystallize as a being educated to the total being, to reach the fullness of existence.

First, we could conclude on the systematization process:

- That it helped to organize, construct and reconstruct events and experiences, favoring the creation of discourses resulting from reflection, analysis and criticism of the process, thus rescuing the lessons learned. To understand how this experience was lived and why it was developed in this way and not in another in order to be able to propose changes in the next courses.

    • For the purposes of this work, systematization is conceptualized as a formative, critical and reflective process of educational and technological practice that allows us to order, classify, analyze and interpret the events experienced through a recoverable and reconstructive practice that favors the personal and professional development of the educated being and to be able to share the experience with other people.

- Of the different epistemological approaches to systematization that we present (1) Historical-dialectical; (2) Dialogical and interactive; (3) Hermeneutic; (4) Of reflexivity and the construction of human experience; and (5) Deconstructive; for this research the fourth epistemological approach was taken as a tool that complements and nourishes the methodological proposal.

- The usefulness of the methodology of the process of systematization of experiences of Jara (2012) became evident, with the five "times" : (1) The starting point: the experience; (2) Formulate a systematization plan; (3) The recovery of the lived process; (4) The background reflections and (5) The points of arrival, to understand, analyze the process and organize how this practical experience was lived to have a healthy life.

Secondly, it should be noted that the facts developed in the training process of the participants in the framework of the DHIPV course were:

- To provide the participant with theoretical and practical tools for a healthy life and awareness of self-respect and respect for others.
- To raise the academic-personal level of the 47 participants selected in the sample of the three (3) nuclei studied (Apure, Maracay and San Juan de los Morros) demonstrated in the quantitative and qualitative analysis carried out in the work.

- The achievement indicator "realizing" in order to *"take charge of"* and relevant behavior is relevant because it allows to evaluate a change of attitude towards an integral conception of education for the design of possible actions of change and transformation in the different scenarios of the context: classroom, family and community.

Thirdly, by reconstructing the experience through the ordered view of the practice and the context within the framework of the DHIPV course, lived by the participants in three nuclei (Apure, Maracay and San Juan de los Morros) in the systematization process, we can conclude:

- The recognition of the participants through the plurality, diversity and richness of the forty-seven (47) experiences and testimonies observed through their reflections and experiences that were captured in the portfolio.

- The integration of reality, the context, situation, environment, and the environment of the lived process, the analysis and reflection that we call it in its totality in the "realization of" in order to "*take charge of*". The latter is determined and oriented by the systems of relationships, functions, thoughts and actions, where the history on which evolved the individual and collective experience of the participants who accompanied each other in the process, both virtually and in the two face-to-face meetings in the three cores, becomes important.

Fourthly, regarding the innovative elements of the systematized experience through the five-times proposal within the framework of the DHIPV course, we find:

- The deschooling of the teaching and learning process of the participants through the exploration of new ways of knowing and learning through the virtual technology platform (Moodle) combined with workshops, two face-to-face meetings at the beginning and end of the course.

  DHIPV, unassisted groups, cooperating teachers, discussion forums and the portfolio were the innovative elements of the experience.

- The result of a merged process of individual and collective reflection that allowed to socialize knowledge, experiences and validate, with the academic community of UNESR, the knowledge learned.

Fifth, the scope and difficulties encountered by the participants during the training experience in the DHIPV course were:

- The evaluation of the educated being, through the portfolio, the permanent critical reflection of the experiences lived in the process, allows the analysis of frequent situations, the construction of new knowledge and to value the daily life of the personal and professional human contexts.

- The experiences and knowledge allowed a comprehensive approach to the different points of view and conceptions assumed by the course participants, without renouncing to the relativization of the discourses according to the circumstances and conditions that limit or define the processes experienced and the changes that took place throughout these eight weeks.

- The results of a process of individual reflection that will allow the socialization of knowledge, experiences and validation of the knowledge learned with the academic community of the UNESR.

- The events that occurred, due to the short time to meet the objectives of the activities proposed in the organization of the two modules and the four learning guides, with their respective activities (17 readings and a film to develop the module I and 17 readings, a video and 2 CDs for reflection) for these eight weeks of the DHIPV course, were very forced and in some occasions it was perceived in the testimonies and experiences that some readings and exercises were not handled in the fulfillment of the activities of the same, especially in Module II, where it was not consolidated, was very forced and in some opportunities it was perceived in the testimonies and experiences the non handling of some readings and exercises in the fulfillment of the activities of the course, especially in Module II, where the proposed objective was not consolidated as reflected in the qualitative analysis of the logical linkage matrix and collected in the interview conducted with the participants in the last face-to-face meeting.

Sixth, explaining the lived process, bringing to light the new knowledge gained during the course experience through the experiences and experiences are proposed from the educational conception of the scope of a praxiological theory[3] as a science of action where it was achieved:

- The integral formation of the being from the development of the educated being to the Total being is given by/from the experiential domain as a way for spiritual growth and for the interaction of the rest of the domains of the educated being.

- Inner experiences are generators of significant learning in connection with daily experiences, since they focus on the experiential domain as the ability to identify situations from the lived experience through self-observation.

- Every process of self-observation is carried out on the basis of the criteria and indicators of a proposal for the development of the self, the axis of the experiential domain.

- The identification of emotions and feelings that arise from contact with reality allows the

---

[3] Praxeological theory "Theory that regroups theoretically and/or experimentally validated educational norms, prescriptions and practices, and habits and customs that merit further investigation. Examples: The stages of elaboration of a project are.... For increasing school success, it is necessary to respect the significant characteristics of the subject. In general, the statements of practical theory or praxeology provide the details concerning a pedagogical practice or the use of a method. They provide the precisions on how to organize the learning of certain objectives for each category of pupils. They explain the modalities of development of such a skill, etc. Praxiological theory determines the practices that will be channeled in an educational system (program, course, model, management, etc.) in order to allow the students to reach the general and specific objectives in a particular school environment. This theory is understood as the "jurisprudence" or the pharmacopoeia of educators, the set of practices and operations judged desirable in an educational system". Legendre, R. (1979, 1981, 2001)

development of skills in the affective and experiential domain.

- The didactic strategy on the human dimension with learning guides is effective when they are structured from a confrontation between theory and the subject's pedagogical and personal praxis, centered on self-observation, with the recognition of limiting beliefs and interactive reflection, applying the axes of human development: openness, reflection and integration.

- The portfolio is an effective strategy for experiential learning by allowing the organization of the results of the investigative, reflective, creative and experiential process of a human development course.

- The identification of daily experiences connected to the notions, concepts and statements of human development explain the intimate connection between the primary elements of being: body, emotion, mind and spirit.

- The integrating axis of the reflective process addresses the power of noticing-taking charge of..., through self-observation and observation of the mind and meditation as a way to quiet the mind, which leads to the development of intuition as a foundation for creativity.

- The evaluation of skills in the development of the educated being's domains requires accumulated time for reflection where both successes and failures must be declared so that they become acquisitions in the subject's formation.

- Evaluation is effective when it is progressive and takes into account capabilities and achievements at various points in time through field diaries, documents, reproductions and testimonies.

- The evaluation process of the levels of human development is evidenced from the identification of the scope of the learning products through the achievement criteria of the process of self-knowledge and self-reflection.

Regarding recommendations:

- Taking into consideration what was stated by the participants and what was observed in the analysis of the logical linkage matrix, it is recommended to extend the course to 16 weeks, and not to eight as planned, and that there should be 5 follow-up visits, and not two, so that the participants can share their experiences with the group not attended and the course facilitator; doubts are clarified, since, within the framework of sensitization and permanent pedagogical follow-up, for the process of change that the teacher should have and thus contribute to the transformation of education, it is considered important: Observe (level of realization), Reflect (understand, accept, appreciate), Design (build, be creative, innovative), Redesign (identify needs), Act (when projects are realized). Under these premises, the reflective act is propitious as the way for a transformational learning that has its effects on the pedagogical task, as proposed by Ceballos (2006), on transformational learning and being educated.

- The educational theory of the Educated Being until achieving the Total Being and the methodology used in the DHIPV course generated valuable learning and practical contributions, for which it is recommended to implement the mentioned course in other Masters at local and regional level and in the UNESR and other institutions that lead to better conditions for the life of the future facilitator and the human being that the country requires.

6.2. Strategies for communicating learning

- This communicative dimension of the systematization of experience is a fundamental and important aspect of this experience for those who direct the education of our institution and the country, therefore, it will be necessary to share with other people and institutions at local, regional, national and Latin American level, the lessons learned in the course and not only remain in those who lived the experience and participated in it.

  - What was learned in this research and the results of the systematization of the experience will be communicated to the authorities of the Regional Nucleus of Advanced Education Caracas, to the Dean's Office of Advanced Education, to the LinFunDo research line and to the coordinator of the Robinsonian Master's program. In this way we will attend to the communicative dimension of systematization.

  - Systematization must be a permanent dimension in our work and an element of joint learning where a connection between theory, praxis, lived and related experiences between thought and action can be observed.

I would like to conclude this chapter with a verse from the song "Sólo el Amor" by Silvio Rodríguez and the lyrics of José Martí 'Lo que debes amar" (What you must love).

You must love the clay that goes in your hands

you must love its sand to the point of madness
and if not, do not undertake it because it will be in vain
only love illuminates what endures
only love turns the clay into a miracle
you must love the time of attempts
you must love the hour that never shines
and if not, do not pretend to touch what is certain
only love engenders wonder
only love manages to ignite what is dead

This led me to the adventure, the challenge and the dream of systematizing the experience of the DHIPV course through my own "practice and theory for other possible worlds" as Jara (2012:1) calls it.

BIBLIOGRAPHIC REFERENCES

Aporte 32 (198? 9). Bogotá: Dimed.

Alboán, Hegoa. Pedro Arrupe Human Rights Institute (2008.). The adventure of systematization. Como mirar y aprender de nuestras prácticas desde nuestras prácticas. Bilbao: El Autor.

Aravena, M. and Zúñiga C. (2002) Sistematización y Evaluación de Experiencias en Educación. Arcis University. Master in Education. Santiago de Chile: Lom ediciones

Barnechea M., González E. and Morgan M. (1998), La producción de conocimiento en sistematización. Lima-Perú: TPS.

Barrera; M (2010) Systematization of experiences and generation of theories. Carcas: Quirón, Sypal

Blesa, R. M. (n.d.) El Poder transformador del "Darse Cuenta". Mimeographed.

Carr and Kemmis, (1994). Teoría crítica de la enseñanza. Barcelona: Martínez Roca.

Ceballos, B. (2003) Neohistorical Diagnosis and the Intervention of Communities. Lobatera Case. Táchira. UPEL.

(2005) Research teacher education as <being educated>. Experiences of professional practice in the area of social sciences. Cenamec Foundation, Caracas. Venezuela.

(2008) La formación del espacio Venezolano: Una propuesta de investigación y la enseñanza de la geografía nacional. Caracas: FEDEUPEL.

(2009) "The experiential domain and spiritual growth in the formation of the teacher as a total being" UPEL (CIDEPD-CIGHMT). Mimeographed.

(2013) Hacia una Didáctica Magna Contemporánea: Experiencia venezolana en la Formación del Educador. Caracas: la Autora. In press.

Chopra D. (1994) The energy within. Video

Clemente, A (1997). Research and systematization of social programs. Volume 4 of Cuadernos de trabajo: Buenos Aires: FICONG.

Dyer, W. (2001). The Power of the Spirit.

Echeverría, R. (1996) Ontología del Lenguaje. Santiago de Chile: Dolmes.

Ende M. (1996) "Carpeta de apuntes", Madrid : Alfaguara.

Evia G. and Gudynas, E. (1993). Ecología social - Manual de metodologías para educadores populares. Madrid: Nuevas ediciones: Editorial Popular .2nd edition

Francke, M. and Morgan, M.L. (1995): "La sistematización: apuesta por la generación de conocimiento a partir de experiencias de promoción". Lima, Escuela para el Desarrollo (www.alforja.or.cr/sistem/biblio.html).

Freire, P. (1979): Pedagogy of the oppressed Garcés, C. (1988). Systematization of popular education experiences. A methodological proposal. Mexico: CREFAL.

Ghiso A. (1998), De la práctica singular al diálogo con lo plural. Aproximaciones a otros tránsitos y sentidos de la Sistematización en épocas de Globalización. Medellín: Funlam.

Guzmán, L (1991). How to systematize methodological experiences with adolescents and young people: Theoretical, methodological and operational guidelines. Programa de Mujeres Adolescentes CEE. Chile: Mimeografiado.

Hleap J. (1995) "School of Villarrica, Systematization of a popular education experience" Cali. University of Valle,

Jara, O (1989). "La evaluación y la sistematización",in La Sistematización en los proyectos de Educación Bogotá: Popular. Editorial Dimensión Educativa.

(1994). To systematize experiences. Costa Rica: Alforja.

(1998). El aporte de la sistematización a la renovación teórico-práctica de los movimientos sociales. Costa Rica : Alforja

(2001). Dilemmas and challenges of systematizing experiences. Centro de Estudios y Publicaciones. Costa Rica: Alforja

(2012). The Systematization of Experiences: Practice and Theory for other possible worlds. Costa Rica: CEP, CEAAL INTERMON-Oxfam.

Kemmis, S. and Carr, W (1995) Action Research and Communicative action: changing teaching practices and the organisation of educational work. Australia: Mimeo material.

Kisnerman, N and Mustieles, D. (1999).Sistematización de la práctica en grupos. Buenos

Aires: Lumen Humanitas.

Legendre, 1983,1993;1995, 1999 Entre l'angoisse et le reve. Montreal: Guérin.

Lókpez de George (1994) "Investigación, Sistematización y Evaluación de las Experiencias Socioeducativas". Caracas: Revista Educación y Ciencias Humanas Year II N° 9.

(2009) Systematization course for community promoters in the Guaire River Sanitation Project, Antímano. Fundación Escuela de Gerencia Comunitaria. Mimeographed.

López C., Martín, J. (2000) Desarrollo humano y práctica docente. Mexico: Trillas,

Mariña, M. (2008) La Educación como factor de poder en el Socialismo Bolivariano: Fundamentos teóricos-conceptual. Fascículo N° 1 Caracas: UNESR.

Mao Tse Tung (1965), Five philosophical theses. Beijing: Foreign Languages.

Martinic, S. (1984) Algunas categorías de análisis para la sistematización. Santiago: CIDE-FLACSO.

(1987) Methodological elements for the systematization of popular education projects. Santiago de Chile: CIDE

(1996) La construcción dialógica de saberes en contextos de educación popular. In Aportes 46. Bogotá: Dimed.

Martinic S and Walker, H. (1987) La reflexión metodológica en el proceso de sistematización de experiencias de educación popular. CIDE. In various authors. La sistematización de proyectos de educación popular. Santiago de Chile: CEAAL.

Maturana, H (1990). Emotions and language in education and politics. Santiago: Colección HACHETTE/COMUNICACIÓN - CED.

Maturana, H and Nisis, Sima (1995). Formación humana y capacitación. Santiago: DOLMEN.

Maturana, H (1997). La objetividad; un argumento para obligar. Santiago de Chile: DOLMEN.

(1997) La formación humana y capacitación, Santiago de Chile: UNICEF.

(1999). Transformación en la Convivencia. Santiago de Chile: DOLMEN.

(2000) Transformación en la convivencia Santiago de Chile: Dolmen.

Maharishi Sadashiva Isham, (2006) Enlightenment, Caracas: Grupo Intenso.

Maharishi Sadashiva Isham, (2006) Ascension, Caracas: Grupo Intenso.

Medina, S.(1994) La Sistematización: Una herramienta para aprender, crecer y transformar. Caracas: CECODAP, El Papagayo.

Mejia, J. (1989) Sistematizar nuestras prácticas Educativas. Bogotá: CINEP.

Mejia M. (1990) La educación popular en los 90. Quito: Cedeco.

Ministry of Popular Power for Communication and Information (MPPCI). Simón Bolívar National Plan 2008-2013 (1999). Líneas Generales del Plan de Desarrollo Económico y Social de la Nación (2007-2013). Caracas: Author.

Osorio J. (1998) "Cruzar la orilla: Debates emergentes sobre los profesionales de la acción social y educativa" Santiago de Chile: CEAAL.

Pakman M, (1996) Constructions of human experience. Barcelona: Gedisa; Vol. 1

Pierola, V. (1999) La sistematización en el trabajo de educación Popular. Bogotá: Dimensión educativa.

United Nations Development Programme (2011). World Human Development Report 1990-2011. Sustainability and equity: A better future for all. Published by the United Nations Development Programme (UNDP).

Quiroz, T and Morgan M. (1988) Acerca de la Sistematización en: La Sistematización de la Práctica: cinco experiencias con sectores populares. Lima: CELATS

Bolivarian Republic of Venezuela (1999) Líneas Generales del Plan de Desarrollo Económico y Social de la Nación 2001 - 2007. Caracas: El Autor

Selener, D. (1996) Documenting, evaluating and learning from our development projects. Manual de Sistematización Participativa. Quito: International Institute of Rural Reconstruction (IIRR).

Systematization of Experiences: a method to promote emancipatory processes (2010). Apuntes de la Cooperativa Centro de estudios para la Educación Popular CEPEP. Caracas: El Perro y la Rana.

Regional Workshop on Planning, Monitoring and Evaluation of the SPFS, September 2003. Guatemala: The author

Tolle, E. (2001) The Power of Now. Madrid: Gaia

Tolle, E. (2003) Practicing the Power of Now. Madrid:Gaia

Tolle, E. (2005) A New Earth. An awakening to the purpose of your life. Bogotá: Grupo Editorial Norma

Simón Rodríguez National Experimental University. (2006) Institutional Document. Postgraduate Dean's Office. Diseño curricular de la Maestría en Educación Robinsoniana. Caracas. Autor.

(1989) Reglamento sobre el Régimen de Estudios de la UNESR: Caracas: El autor.

Verger, A. (2003). Systematization of experiences. Barcelona: Department of Sociology, University of Barcelona.

Walsh, R. (2000) Espiritualidad esencial. Mexico: Alamah

ANNEXES

Annex A
COURSE: INTEGRAL HUMAN DEVELOPMENT FOR LIFE

LEARNING MODULES I

Dr. Beatriz Ceballos García
Dr. Maritza Puertas

INVITATION TO ADVENTURE...

We welcome you to begin this wonderful adventure: discovering the essence of your being and acting from the transcendence of having been born human. We wish you the greatest of success and remind you to keep in mind the key factors for the achievement of your objectives:

- Commitment as the energy you put into achieving what you want to achieve
- Attendance at general meetings
- Interactive on-line connection
- Creation of learning guides
- Individual and joint reflection in the working groups
- Request support from process facilitators

We invite you, on this journey, to take the helm of your own learning....Read with this story in detail:

THE LIFE YOU HOLD IS IN YOUR HANDS

A group of children knew a wise man in their
village and hatched a plan to trick him.
They would catch a live bird and go to visit the
Wise man.
One of them would hold the bird behind his
back and ask him:
Wise man, is the bird alive or dead?
If the wise man answered that it was alive, the
child would quickly crush the bird and say:
No, it is dead.
If the wise man said: The bird is dead, the
child would show him the bird alive.
The children got the wise man to receive them.

The one holding the bird asked him:
Wise man, is the bird alive or dead?
The wise man remained silent for a few
moments. Then he bent down until he was at the
same height as the boy and said:
<The life you hold is in your hands.

(Selection and adaptation by Beatriz Ceballos. Source: Patricia Hashuel "Conversando con un coach, No 1, October, 1999)

We would like to hear from you: what did you notice?

MODULE I
"THE INTEGRAL FORMATION OF THE BEING FROM THE DEVELOPMENT OF THE EDUCATED BEING TO THE TOTAL BEING".

Our objectives, during the first two weeks, will be guided by the following questions:

J **How to integrate my domains (cognitive-conceptual, affective, physical, social, perceptual, moral and experiential) of the educated self towards the formation of the total self?**

J **How do the axes (openness, reflection and integration) of human development participate in my integral formation?**

J **What are my competencies as a "learner" towards the integration of the primary elements of being: body, mind, emotion and spirit?**

J **How do I observe, accept and re-create the essence of the human being I discover in myself?**

LEARNING GUIDE NO. 1

INTRODUCTION

Welcome to this space for learning! We will share this meeting from the emotionality of enthusiasm and joy. This invitation is oriented towards the possibility of enjoying the pleasure of "realizing" as observers of ourselves and others. We offer you a series of activities, which will support your growth as you choose to walk through the unknown, *letting go of* all the ties that provide the so-called "enemies of learning" and cultivating our allies. We wish you much success!

STARTING THE GAME...

We invite you to watch the film "The Dead Poets Society" (**Annex 1**).

We only ask you to keep a self-observation of emotions, sensations and judgments. In particular, become aware of the so-called "private conversations". Private conversation is realized as a thought that arises when we judge what we are hearing directly or indirectly without sharing it... We suggest that you stop the movie for approximately every half hour.

- Proceed to organize your reflections in a text based on the following aspects and those that arise spontaneously:

   - Your emotions (joy, anger, sadness, fear...) sensations and judgments.

   - what do you discover about yourself... as a parent... as a professional?
     As a member of the community where you live?

- Formulate questions about teacher-student, parent-child, and community relationships that you think the film answers. For example, one question that we are sure the film answers is: How can the teacher make learning more effective for the student?

I.   Self-observation and self-help

1.1 Observe your breathing: We invite you to acquire the skill and habit of breathing and quieting your mind. it will surely be a pleasant experience. do it fully. have fun!

Select a half hour a day that you consider conducive to you. Make it a quiet place. You can take a few gentle breaths from the base of your lungs, following these instructions: Inhale through the nose very slowly (in three beats), hold the air for three seconds, then exhale through the mouth slowly (three seconds).You rest three seconds to exhale again and repeat this cycle several times. Then you begin to observe the mind moving.let the thoughts flow.observe it without trying.without straining.with perfect innocence...just observe.you will naturally contact that space of peace.rest there.if some thoughts come to you.it's ok.don't dwell on them.

Make a brief report on your experience: write about your sensations, emotions...

1.2 Watch your walk: pay attention to how you walk for at least five minutes a day. Pay attention to the way you move. How do your arms sway; your shoulders; are they forward or backward? Where does your head and gaze stay? On which legs do you put the most weight? How is your stride? How is your rhythm? When you stand up you become aware of the shape your body takes, its tendencies; posture, where do you exert yourself the most effort? For a second, exaggerate those tendencies as intensely as possible. Draw yourself in those postures and record the answers to these questions: What emotions arise when you stand exaggerating your tendencies for a while? What characteristics can your corporeality have in the years to come if you recurrently maintain those tendencies?

Make a short report about your experience: write about your sensations, emotions, tell us what you discover about yourself through this exercise.

II. Individual reading and reflection

2.1 We invite you to read the material entitled: "El poder de darse cuenta" by Blesa, R. M. (n.d.). **(Annex 2).**

Record your impressions from the following questions:

- What emotions, sensations and judgments arose in you?

- Take the time to answer the questions proposed in the text, incorporating the **indicators or evidence** of your answer: Am I being what I want to be? Am I doing what I want to do? Am I having what I want to have? Am I giving and receiving what I want to give and receive? Am I at peace with my past? Am I living fully and consciously my present? Am I building "here and now" the foundations of the future I want for myself? Is my life respecting my harmony, that of others and the environment?

- In the event that you answer some questions negatively, with the corresponding evidence, what actions can you take (take charge) so that your answers are always positive?

- She extracts at least three theoretical postulates from the author's conception of conscious or transformational learning.

- Design some actions that will bring you closer and closer to the ability to "notice".

2.2 We invite you to read the fourth part (The formation of the teacher as an integral being) of the book: Formación del espacio venezolano. A proposal for research and teaching of national geography" Ceballos, B., 2008 **(Annex 3).** We will divide the reading in three parts fundamentally. For each of them we propose some questions that invite you to reflect. You are not obliged to answer each question; you can organize your discourse to cover all of them and even add approaches inspired by this reflective process.

Part One (pp.199 - 208)
- How do you think you can exercise the axes of human development: Openness, Reflection and Integration? Point out some concrete actions.
- Based on the scope of each domain of the educated being, elaborate a list of actions that as a teacher you would carry out in each of these domains.

- What advantages do you infer the application of the principles of transformational or conscious learning would have? Also take into consideration the proposal of the observer, action and results model.

Part Two (pp. 216-218)

- The experiential domain is the axis of the development of the rest of the domains of the educated being. Identify the value of the development of the social domain from the experiential domain as a way to foster values of solidarity, responsibility and commitment. What strikes you about the approach in relation to the development of the social being and its connection with the experiential domain?

Part Three (pp. 219-230)

- What emotions do Maturana's educational approaches emerge in you? To what extent have you considered in your educational praxis the intimate relationship between the primary elements of being? You can read some theoretical statements about the same author incorporated in this module **(Annex 4).**
- What actions can you take to change the results from the application of these approaches?
- What is the value of the development of the experiential domain in the transcendence of the human being?

2.3 . There are times when our learning is blocked by limiting beliefs or judgments that have been called "enemies of learning" whose content is found in **Annex 5**.We invite you to listen to and/or read the poem "Romance de mi niña mala" (**Annex 6)** Proceed to record the following:

- Identify the enemies of the neighbor's learning of ingenuity.
- Identifies the traits of the educated being possessed by the teacher of the Girl.
- Identify which learning enemies are present in you and in what intensity (on a scale of 1 to 10).
- Formulate some actions to change the results of your behaviors in relation to these "enemies".

III.   Recording of specific exercises

3.1   We invite you to watch again the movie: "The Dead Poets Society".
Select at least three characters to answer the following questions:

- What situations of the characters do you identify that move away or come closer to the practice of the traits of the total being, especially the Being of Love, Being of Autonomy and Being of Authenticity? Record it in writing

- What are the indicators of each of these traits of the total self that you identify in yourself? At what level: high, medium or low?

To carry out this activity you will be supported by the following reading: Total Being in chapter VII of the work of Legendre, Renald, Entre l'angoisse et le reve. Montreal: Guérin, 1993, pp. 185-241. **(Appendix 7)**

3.2   Optional Activity: Let's play! Imagine that you are a famous pedagogue of international stature. You have been invited to the XV International Congress of New Paradigms in Education to be held in Australia, to speak about the Total Being model. Prepare in two pages the fundamental ideas that you will expose at that time..... Good luck!...it will be an honor for you to represent our country in such an important event.

IV.   Acting to transcend

Based on the reflective process you have developed in this guide, we invite you to formulate some actions that will allow you to achieve the desired results in your teaching practice and in the family and community environment.

Finally, we would like to know what you think of the following statement:

LIFE WAS MEANT TO BE LIVED IN ETERNAL JOY,
UNCONDITIONAL LOVE, ABSOLUTE FREEDOM AND UNLIMITED AWARENESS. ANYTHING
LESS IS ABSOLUTELY MISSING
THE POINT OF BEING BORN HUMAN (MSI).
We congratulate you for giving yourself the permission to start this journey towards
becoming the total being!
BC/MP, Caracas, Caracas, November 2008

LEARNING GUIDE NO. 2

INTRODUCTION

I congratulate you on your decision to continue consolidating your learning. You gave yourself the opportunity to develop this guide that we hope will bring you much pleasure and of course happiness. This guide deepens in a fundamental competence in every conscious learning process: SELF-observation, the beautiful process of "noticing" and reflecting on ourselves and what happens to us in the experience of living. This time, we will appreciate the relationships between language, corporeality and emotions that define our actions. We invite you to float, to let go, to feel the wonder of becoming aware of each moment lived with the sole purpose of deepening our human condition from the lightness. Go ahead, in your hands is the path of transcendence of the educated being towards the total being!

Your openness is the first step to let yourself be "bathed" in the new, to learn and unlearn and achieve your dreams Are you still willing to walk this path of gentleness... of love?

WE CONTINUE THE GAME...

Select a quiet space to listen to the poem "Décima del tiempo .tiempo" (**Appendix 8**). Listen (hear, interpret and appreciate) without expectations, innocently.

Proceeds to:

- Record emotions and private conversations that you already know how to identify.

- Now you can support yourself with the text written about "Enemies of learning".

(**Appendix 9**). Record your self-observation: which enemies of learning do you identify in each part of the poem? what would be the indicators of openness to learning? According to **Appendix 10**, do you recognize these enemies and/or indicators of openness in yourself? Remember that the importance of "noticing" is that you can "take charge of".

- Choose some "indicators of openness to learning" that allow you to make commitments to yourself, to your family, to your friends and to the members of a community to which you belong. What actions have you taken or would you take?

- Up to this point: How do you feel? What would you like to communicate? It is important to stay aware of what is happening to us and to put it out there... beautiful steps of humility.... ...gateway to *absolute freedom*.

IV.   Self-observation and self-help

4.1 . Observe your breathing and walking: We invite you to continue practicing daily the observation of your breathing and walking as explained in the first guide. You can report the experience you have had.

4.2 Observe yourself during some meals of the day: make a daily record of what you notice: How do you feel when you eat? How fast do you eat? What flavors do you perceive? What do you think about while you eat? What emotions do you contact? How do you chew your food?

V.   Individual reading and reflection

We selected Maturana to expand the human sense in education. Read carefully the selected material from the book: *Transformation in coexistence*, on pages 62 to 73 (**Annex 11**). We only ask you to write a paragraph containing a thought of your own that has arisen from the inspiration of the author's analysis proposals.Suddenly.you create some ideas that will make you famous or famous in the educational field for its deeply human sense.Imagine how proud you would feel to contribute with the thought of a transforming education! *Congratulations in advance...*

VI.   Recording of specific exercises

6.1 I invite you to delve deeper into the relationship between emotions/language/corporeality with the following selected material:

6.2 Analyze **annex 12** of the document entitled "Strategies for the formation of the educated being as a transformational leader (Ceballos, 2005). Perform the exercises on page 5.

6.3 Read the selection on "listening" (**Annex 13**: pp. 136-174), judgments (**Annex 14**: pp.101-133), and types of conversations (**Annex 15**: pp. 217-245), from Echeverría's work "The Ontology of Language". Proceed to observe several family and professional situations, in order to identify actions that would validate the arguments contained in the selected readings. Record your findings in writing.

6.4 Watch your favorite novel for a week or a rented movie (we recommend some titles: Devil's advocate, Contact, Life is beautiful, The red mill, Harry Potter or others, you can even use the movie "The dead poets society" and identify two characters (those who act more) and record their emotions, their judgments and the corporality they assume. To do this, read carefully the contents of the chart on the relationship between emotions/ corporality, organized from Maturana's work "Biology of love" (**appendix 16).

FEATURES	EMOTIONS	JUDGMENTS	CORPORALITY
	Write down the basic emotions you observe: joy, anger, sadness, fear. You can expand the identification with the last chart that appears in this material on emotions (appendix 16).	Write down **verbatim** the judgments made and the so-called private conversations that you can infer from it. corporeality of each character. Remember that it is not your interpretation.	You can keep in mind: -Posture -Gestures -Tone of voice -Voice intonation -Facial expression - Type of gaze -Muscle tension

6.5 Record your observations in the following table as shown below:

4.1 Once you have read the selected material on Echeverría's "The Promises" (**appendix 17),** formulate the promises that you intend to fulfill in this course, in different periods of time.

4.2 **Optional Activity:** After talking about the scope of an education centered on the self, you will undoubtedly have many things to say. We offer you a space to produce a three-page essay, where you will critically show a synthesis of your most significant learning as a teaching professional, committed to an education for life...Success! ...could it be published?...Why not? Don't stop...they are waiting for you. You can start it right now, but you can submit it at any time before the end of the course.

Finally, if you have anything to add in relation to this sentence, it would be welcome!!!!

LIFE WAS MADE TO BE LIVED IN ETERNAL JOY,
UNCONDITIONAL LOVE, ABSOLUTE FREEDOM AND UNLIMITED AWARENESS.
ANYTHING LESS THAN THAT IS MAKING YOU
ABSOLUTELY MISS THE POINT OF BEING BORN HUMAN (MSI).

We congratulate you for giving yourself the permission to **continue on** this path towards the conformation of the total being!

BC/MP, Caracas, Caracas, November 2008

Annex B

MODULE II

THE DEVELOPMENT OF THE EXPERIENTIAL DOMAIN OF THE EDUCATED BEING AS A PATH TO SPIRITUAL GROWTH.

Our objectives during the last two weeks will be guided by the following questions:

J **How to quiet the mind?**

J **How to deepen the power of now?**

J **What can we do to expand our consciousness and recognize our essence?**

J **How to flow with the external world from inner wisdom?**

LEARNING GUIDE NO. 3

INTRODUCTION

We congratulate you for your decision to continue consolidating your learning and consolidation of the total being. We continue to choose as a common thread: SELF-OBERVATION. Now, we are going to deepen in the relationships between language, corporeality and emotions in connection with the spiritual. The development of the experiential domain as the axis of spirituality will be the center of the proposed exercises. Keep enjoying....becoming more and more aware of your nature as a total being that you are fully recognizing in yourself. Keep playing big ... *"Absolute freedom is closer than your next breath".*

WE CONTINUE THE GAME...

- Select a quiet space to listen to "The Song of the Cicadas" (**Appendix 18**).

• What emotions come up in you? Anger?...joy?...anger?...sadness?...frustration?

• Now, you can read the text (**see appendix 3**. p.229) Re-identify your emotions and the judgments that arise in you with each emotion. Record these emotions and the "private conversations" that accompany them.

• What actions can you take to change the results of the behaviors described in the song? We recommend you to read Maturana's work: "Human formation and training", pages 17 to 22. (**Annex 19**) You will be able to identify the impact on the child's life when *being rather than doing is corrected.*

• Now we invite you to act from love. Maturana offers us in this We selected one of the following workshops: 1, 2, 3, 5, and 7 (Annex 20). Select one of the following workshops: 1, 2, 3, 5, and 7 (**Annex 20), in** order to apply it with a group of students, colleagues, family or friends. Visualize the workshop so that you can flow with the experience. In addition, you can consult the text "Mastering the patristic culture" contained in the material entitled "Strategies for the formation of the educated being as a transformational leader (Ceballos, 2005). (**Annex 21**).

• **Note**: if you wish to choose another workshop, different from the one selected by us, you can do it.

VII. Self-observation

1.1 **Observe your breathing and walking:** We invite you to continue practicing daily the observation of your breathing and walking as explained in the first guide. You can report the experience you have had.

1.2 **Observe your mind:** We will delve into the recognition of the space of peace that resides in every human being. You will do it with the use of a technique of observing the mind. We invite you to do some exercises in a quiet place. First, take several breaths, as we taught you in guide No. 1. Once relaxed, follow the instructions below:

1. *Counting thoughts*
Once relaxed, close your eyes and begin to observe and count the thoughts. Don't look for anything to happen and don't try to change anything you are observing. Take just two minutes. Slowly open your eyes, answer: Was it easy? How many thoughts did you count? Were you able to be alert or aware of your thoughts?

2. *Observing the mind without counting, without doing anything, just observing*
You can do this for two minutes. Were you able to observe? Were there spaces between thoughts, moments of silence or space? Was it easy?

Record all your experiences. Only when you are finished can you read **attachment 22**: "Talk on Observing the Mind" by Manyu, unified consciousness teacher of Ishayas Ascension. Extract the main ideas and make a commentary based on the experience you had with the exercise.

VIII. Individual Reading and Reflection

2.1 Love is the universal force that allows everything to flow in harmony. We are beings of love... do you remember what you knew of the total being, as a being of love? Always in connection with the autonomous being and authentic being. These traits are consolidated as you deepen as a being of spirituality, which involves connecting with your inner energy.the space of peace, love and stillness that resides within us. Now we invite you to reflexively access some arguments about love. To do this, we offer you a selection from the work entitled "Ascension" between page 25-35 **(Appendix 23).** Record your answers to the following questions:

-       From the reflections made on your self-observation and observations about your present and the content of this reading, respond briefly:
-       What judgments, emotions, and body patterns limit you? What would be the most important ones?
possible reasons?
-       Which ones make it possible for you?
-       What aspects of yourself do you want to keep?
-       What aspects do you want to change?

\-   What actions can you take to change the undesired results?

\-   With the material on the Total Being, we invite you to read again the part referring to the *being of spirituality*, from Annex 7, then the final part of this chapter which is attached to this guide: "And always happiness? (**Annex 24**).

\-   Observe the judgments, emotions and body postures you adopt.
during the reading. Record them. Remember the intimate connection that exists between body, mind, emotions and spirit. Recognizing them is an important phase to advance in the identification of your essence from the experiential domain. Look at the chart entitled: Developmental Domains and Constitutive Subsystems of the Human Being (Appendix 25).

IX.   Recording of specific exercises

9.1.   You realized the role of the experiential domain in our growth as total beings. Now, we invite you to carry out with a group of students, colleagues, friends or relatives the workshop N°11, among the following: 13, 14, 15, 16 and 17 of Maturana's work: "Human formation and training". (**Annex 26**). Visualize the workshop so that you can identify and flow with the experience. Record what you noticed in relation to the development of the experiential domain. What struck you the most? **Note**: if you wish to choose another workshop, different from the one we selected, you may do so.

9.2.   Bravo! You have come to develop the power of "realizing" which is the prelude to recognition of your essence. In the next guide you will be able to better understand what we mean when we talk about the "essence of who we are". For now, we just invite you to flow, to observe what you experience, without labeling...

9.3.   The state of consciousness that you must be acquiring at this moment can allow you to advance in a concept of happiness and spirituality with your own words, you can support yourself with the readings. Thank you for this contribution. it emerges from gentleness, without much explanation, "from the source rather than from your mind". Later you will be able to deepen in the meaning of this last expression.

9.4.   The following activity should be done **only after the previous one**. What we are looking for is for you to develop the ability to "realize" from the experiential domain. Proceed to read the material on: *Spirituality and Expansion of Consciousness* (Internet selection - **Annex 27**) and from Roger Walsh's work "Essential Spirituality", pp. 13-37 (optional consultation) **Annex 28.** Proceed to record the following:

> - Keep in mind the concepts you formulated above in your own words. Contrast them with the information in these references. Can you point out the aspects that coincide and those that you would add in a next formulation? Very good!... that is flowing... being innocent... accessing the understanding... from the experience .... How do you feel at this moment? What is your experience?

X. **Acting to transcend:** Proposes an activity whose realization evidences the transcendence of what has been learned.

LIFE WAS MADE TO BE LIVED IN ETERNAL JOY,
UNCONDITIONAL LOVE, ABSOLUTE FREEDOM AND UNLIMITED AWARENESS.
ANYTHING LESS THAN THAT IS MAKING YOU
ABSOLUTELY MISS
THE POINT OF BEING BORN HUMAN (MSI).

We congratulate you for giving you the permission to **continue** this path towards the conformation of the
total being. towards your absolute freedom!

BC/MP, Caracas, Caracas, November 2008

MODULE II

THE DEVELOPMENT OF THE EXPERIENTIAL DOMAIN OF THE EDUCATED BEING AS A PATH TO SPIRITUAL GROWTH.

Our objectives, during the last two weeks, will be guided by the following questions:

J **How to quiet the mind?**

J **How to deepen the power of now?**

J **What can we do to expand our consciousness and recognize our essence?**

J **How to flow with the external world from inner wisdom?**

LEARNING GUIDE NO. 4

INTRODUCTION

We are very happy to know that your level of consciousness is increasing... If you have done the activities as we have suggested, and if not and you have done them with gentleness, lightness and innocence, **surely** your progress is exponential. You have already tasted the fullness of total being. You have already experienced that space of love, peace and stillness that resides in each one of us. You no longer judge yourself frequently for what you do, you simply reflect on the next action to change the results. You are no longer aware that you are not your thoughts, that you are *pure consciousness*. You no longer identify yourself with thoughts.emotions. Ah!!!...You may go into great anger.sadness.rage.fear..., but you don't identify with it. If the emotion comes.you just let it be.you observe it.you let it flow.you let it go.and peace invades your heart.Everything is so easy. The secret is to choose for that space that is your essence. Sometimes your mind gets in your way and you start to listen and pay attention to some voices: "I can't stop my mind", "I won't be able to do it until I do this or that", "I'll never achieve my spiritual growth", "I'll never achieve my spiritual growth", "I'll never achieve my spiritual growth". "I will never achieve my spiritual growth"..... "this is impossible" etc. etc. etc. This is just the sabotage of the mind.you are a limitless being.infinite.the choice is for the *present* moment. If we take on the *power of the now*. our level of consciousness will grow into joy.infinite love and peace. are you excited for us to continue. All right! That's playing big!

If at this moment a genie appears to you with the capacity to grant you one wish, just one. what would be the greatest wish of your life? do you want peace? love? wisdom? freedom? inner growth? whatever wish comes from your heart will be granted. just wish for it. From now on, make it conscious so that it will be the north of your actions. This last guide will provide you with the tools and principles to achieve it. Remember the phrase that has accompanied us all the time.

LIFE WAS MADE TO BE LIVED IN ETERNAL JOY,
UNCONDITIONAL LOVE, ABSOLUTE FREEDOM AND UNLIMITED CONSCIOUSNESS.
ANYTHING LESS THAN THAT IS
ABSOLUTELY MISSING
THE POINT OF BEING BORN HUMAN (MSI).
WE CONTINUE THE GAME...

You will remember from the first guide that understanding comes naturally from experience.

Therefore, our invitation is to play from experience. This phrase that has accompanied us, you have already lived it, perhaps only for a few hours, minutes or seconds. It doesn't matter. What matters is that you have realized that everything arises in you when you focus on it. it arises from the source. How can you prolong that experience of peace? One way is through *meditation*. The reason is very obvious, we were not taught to look within. then we forget that we were born with that energy within. we forget that we are that. that is our birthright. Now what we want to give you is a way to install a new habit: to look inward to have a new experience of permanent peace and joy.

With the help of a CD on meditation made by D. Chopra (**Annex 29**) you will find a quiet place, place yourself in a comfortable position, preferably seated. Listen attentively to the CD and let yourself be "bathed" by the instructions. At the end report your experience at the very moment it ends...don't go to the past. Start with the present...Then you can report how your process went: Was it easy? What were the initial emotions and judgments? Become aware of how that ingrained habit of looking only outward caused you to stop having attention in that space of inner peace and stillness.

There are several types of meditation: Transcendental meditation, Zen, Kundalini, Shamadi, the Ascension of the Ishayas. We consider the use of the techniques of the Ascension of the Ishayas to be very powerful. They are based on the fundamental principles of Praise, Gratitude and Love, taking us inward in an extremely gentle way for the body and mind. See **Appendix 30.** We also invite you to consult the website: www.caminobrillante.com. Select the entry: introductory talks. Proceed to listen to them attentively. Record your impressions, establishing a connection with the learning you have obtained up to this point.

You can expand (optional) your knowledge of the types of meditation with the selected material (**Annex 31**):

- What is the central purpose of these types of meditation?
- What actions can you take to get into the habit of meditating frequently?

1.   Self-observation

1.3 **Observe your breathing and walking:** We invite you to continue practicing daily the observation of your breathing and walking as explained in the first guide. Have you had any change? We would like to know your experience. It is only a pretext to develop self-observation in you.

1.4 **Learning the ways of nature:** Continue practicing breathing exercises, relaxation, visualization. Now we invite you to develop self-knowledge by identifying in yourself the elements of nature:

earth, fire, water and air. To what extent is there a balance? You can exercise in *these through* some activities suggested in a CD (**Annex 32**), follow the instructions properly. If you can do it in a group and have someone to help you record the answers to the questions, the exercise will be much more effective.

1.5 Now you can read **appendix 33**, entitled: *"Learning the ways of nature"*. It is convenient that this reading is not done before the exercise, in order to perform it innocently. Afterwards, you can direct it to a group of students or other people. It will help you to make distinctions to deepen your self-observation process.

The exercises you performed on the elements of nature allowed you to identify those that define you and those that are not very present in you. Become aware of this situation and incorporate more strongly the weaker ones and reduce those that are too developed. Seek balance between these elements. Become aware of when it is more convenient to show one with respect to the other. Record your experience.

XI. Individual Reading and Reflection

...My experience at this moment is one of total happiness...of plenitude...joy...to perceive the energy that flows from my being in each exercise that I propose to you.in each selection of readings.of activity. The emotion that flows in my being is of joy.immense joy..total surrender.choosing for that space of peace.of silence.full presence with what I am.pure consciousness.infinite.source of all existence.(December 08, 2008, at 11:00 am)

We wanted to share an individual experience with you in this present, an example of what we can experience from the now. Well, that's what this part of the guide is all about. First you are going to read two parts of Tolle's "Practicing the Power of Now". (**Appendix 34**). Report what you find most significant about each part of the reading, using the suggested questions.

Remember that everything is a game...don't take anything seriously...that's giving power to the mind...when you get serious you are judging...so have fun!!!!!

Part One: (pp. 1-49 and pp. 93-108)

- What is your experience of observing the observer?

- On you: What are the benefits of the enlightened state that you have experienced at some point? Remember that we are enlightened beings... It is our birthright; what we lack is to make it conscious all the time.

- What is your experience when you choose for the present moment... for the now? Record what you experienced when doing the exercises or in another moment in everyday life.

- What is your experience when you observe an emotion?

Part Two: (pp. 121-139)

Your social being is expanded when relationships with others emerge from that space of love.when you begin to be compassionate with yourself and then with others. Your capacity to guide your family, your friends, the members of your local community is deepened when you do it from unconditional love and wisdom. MSI said, *"Define your life in terms of what you can do for others. If you want your life only for yourself, it will be small. If you want to heal, enrich and enlighten the world, then your life will be enriched, long and wonderful. Each day will bring more joy than the last."*

- What is your experience of practicing compassion with yourself and others?
- What can you do to change the undesired results in a given situation?
- What can you do to maintain the desired results?
- What have been your experiences of acceptance and surrender?
- What has been your practice of compassion with your family, friends and members of the community where you participate?

Finally, we invite you to read MSI's work "Ascension", pages 36-54, (**Appendix 35**) where you can reflect on the need for the ***death of the ego*** and the ***expansion of love*** and make a comment from your own experience.

CONGRATULATIONS....!!! We are "hopping on one leg "...we are sure that if you carried out these instructions you are enjoying an enlightening experience that fills us with optimism about the destiny of education in the

esciiela...of your performance with your family, friends and your community...It is cultivating peace from every act of our life...Isn't it beautiful.hopeful?

XII. Recording of specific exercises

3.3. We suggest you make contact to initiate the practice of yoga. We are aware of the short time available for this practice. We only invite you to register the importance of this practice that you can extract from the material in **appendix 36.** Remember that your body is very wise...when you can practice little by little these stretching exercises will give the flexibility to your body in a way that will help you to expand your inner experience. You are just remembering your nature. You don't have to look for anything. Everything is in you...discover it.make it conscious.that's all.

3.4. The practice of yoga promotes meditation. It contributes to go beyond the limitations imposed by the mind, proper to the awakened state of consciousness. We invite you to understand the scope of the four states of consciousness that overcome the limitations of our existence. The states of consciousness are the different ways in which we experience life: awake, sleeping, dreaming as ordinary states of consciousness. The extraordinary states of consciousness are pointed out by MSI in his work "Ascension" (**Appendix 37** - pp. 156-177) These are: ascending state of consciousness, perpetual ascending consciousness or beginning of enlightenment, exalted ascending consciousness and unified consciousness or absolute enlightenment. After the reading answer the following questions:

- What are the indicators or evidences to identify the state of ascending consciousness, perpetual ascending consciousness or beginning of enlightenment, exalted ascending consciousness and unified consciousness or absolute enlightenment?

3.4. The knowledge of the Yoga Sutras of Patanjali guide us towards a life practice that allows us to overcome the state of awakened consciousness. We invite you to read MSI's work: "Enlightenment" (**appendix 38**) where you will be able to identify the scope of the benefits of choosing to stay in the now... in the infinite peace that is our spiritual essence. Read between pages: 1 to 15:

- What judgments, emotions and corporeality arise in you?
- What prevents you from achieving enlightenment?
- Do you have any questions you would like to present at our face-to-face meeting?

· **I. Acting to Transcend (Optional Activity)**

We invite you to enjoy another gift. Select a quiet place, if you can be with another participant of the course, it will be fun to share with each other. Now proceed to watch the video of D. Chopra, (**Appendix 39**) entitled: *"The energy within"*. We suggest you start watching it without expectations, innocently. You can do the breathing exercises that help you to relax. Surely you will understand the content little by little and if doubts arise simply accept it with gentleness, without judging. Surely you could appreciate the author's arguments in relation to concepts such as: *energy, time/space, present, pure consciousness, attention/intention, spirit/soul, experience of silence or unitary consciousness, Universe, observed/thinker, body/mind, observer/thinker, enlightenment*. You can stop the video before the end to clarify some ideas, rather than to understand absolutely everything. Perhaps there will be things that you cannot understand because you have not experienced them. So don't worry, we will help you to deepen your experience in the face-to-face session. Record the answers to the following questions: We suggest the following sub-parts or tracks: 5, 6, 10, 12, 13 and 14.

- Which approach or approaches did you find most interesting?

- Stop at the part of the video where he explains the importance of that space between thought and thought. Exercise, focus on that space, as you have been given the instruction. That space of peace.stillness.is the source.the infinite.the ascendant. Gently pay your attention in this space is the key to *freedom...absolute enlightenment*.

With the experience you have had with the practice of meditation and the reflections arising from Chopra's video, answer: What value do you assign to meditation as it relates to spiritual growth?

If questions or doubts arise, you can share them in the classroom session.

Annex C

INITIATION WORKSHOP FOR DHIPV COURSE FACILITATORS: TOWARDS THE IMPLEMENTATION OF A NEW EDUCATIONAL PARADIGM BASED ON HUMAN DEVELOPMENT

Dr. Maritza Puertas
Dr. Beatriz Ceballos García

March, 2009

Introduction

The Human Development for Life course is aimed at *Human Transformation supported by theoretical and methodological principles on human development that contribute to the formation of a professional with an individual and collective conscience towards their own transformation and education.* This scope makes it an experiential course, where the axis of its development is constituted by the participants' own experiences. The learning modules are organized with activities where the relationship between the elements of being: body, emotions, mind and spirit, become the axis to discover the level of individual and collective consciousness.

It is considered necessary to reinforce the reflective process of the experiences lived by the participants through direct meetings with those responsible for the course, but previously to guarantee a meeting or support with participating teachers who will have an empowerment to guide the production of the learning modules. This empowerment process will begin with this initiation workshop.

The theoretical and methodological context of the workshop can be extracted from the preliminary program attached to this document. The general program of the workshop allows us to appreciate the scope of this empowerment and the didactic strategies that would accompany the monitoring process of the group of participating teachers interested in supporting this initiative.

Purpose:

To develop basic skills in a group of participating teachers to support the delivery of the learning modules designed for the *human development for life course.*

Specific objectives:

1. To reflect on the conceptions of the new educational paradigm and possible strategies to achieve the formation of the total being.

2. Identify the educational value of the situation between the Observer's domains: body, emotions-language and spirit and the axes of human development.

3. Recognize the pedagogical criteria that support the strategies designed to create the conditions that allow participants to expand their capacity for action and reflection in the world where they live, in order to contribute to its conservation and transformation in a responsible manner with the environment where they live.

Contents:

- New educational paradigm based on human development
- Transformational learning
- Observer, action and outcome model
- The Observer's domains: body, emotions-language and spirit.
- The domains of being educated and being whole and the axes of human development

Work strategies

Phase I: Initiation of reflection

- General justification of the activity
- Reflective conversations on the traits of the total self and the enemies of learning.
- Exercises on the principles of the new educational paradigm

Phase II: Transformational learning and the process of realization

- Interactive dialogue on the Observer Model, Action and Outcome and Observer Domains

- Development of exercises on the relationship between the elements of being and the axes of human development.

Phase III: The transcendence of learning

- Reflections on teaching and the demands of the new educational paradigm.

- Development of exercises based on the experiences of the application of the pedagogical principles of the course proposal.

HUMAN AND MATERIAL RESOURCES

Coordinators:

Dr. Maritza Puertas
Dr. Beatriz Ceballos García
Support Facilitator: Nersa Colmenares

General terms and conditions

Two days: Friday and Saturday
Timetable: twelve on-site and eight off-site hours

Caracas, March 2009

Annex D

PROPOSAL FOR THE INDUCTION OF FACILITATORS TO
DEVELOP THE WORKSHOP FOR THE IMPLEMENTATION OF THE PROGRAM OF
THE
INTEGRAL HUMAN DEVELOPMENT FOR LIFE COURSE.

Beatriz Ceballos Dr. Maritza
Puertas Dr. Maritza Puertas
April/2009

Introduction:

The nature of this course makes it necessary to hold a workshop for its implementation among the participants. We consider it important to orient the team of facilitators. For this purpose, we propose the implementation of some activities by the whole team in order to contribute to the successful development of this course. The proposal is based on the experience we had in the induction course held in February of this year, where only four of the facilitators of the team that was finally formed were able to attend. The general program of the implementation workshop is included, which will be sent to the participants in order to guarantee their attendance to a face-to-face session, if time is available for a session of at least three hours.

Proposal:

Part One: Facilitators' experiences

The development of the initial face-to-face workshop of the DHIPV course by the facilitators requires that each of them experience at least some of the proposed strategies to guarantee a better conduction of the program implementation process. The criteria for this decision making is the experiential nature of the course, based on self-observation, reflection and integration of learning to transcend as a total being.

Develop the following strategies contained in the learning guides before having the face-to-face workshop to implement the course syllabus:

First strategy: Observing the mind

Observe your breathing: We invite you to acquire the skill and habit of breathing and quieting your mind..... .it will surely be a pleasant experience'...realize it fully...

...have fun!!!!

1) Select a half hour a day that you consider conducive to you. Make it a quiet place. You can take a few gentle breaths from the base of your lungs, following these instructions: Inhale through the nose very slowly (in three beats), hold the air for three seconds, then exhale through the mouth slowly (three seconds).You rest three seconds to exhale again and repeat this cycle several times. Then you begin to observe the mind moving.let the thoughts flow.observe it without trying.without straining.with perfect innocence...just observe.you will naturally contact that space of peace.rest there.if some thoughts come to you.it's ok.don't dwell on them.

2) How to quiet the mind

3) *Counting thoughts*

   Once relaxed, close your eyes and begin to observe and count the thoughts. Don't look for anything to happen and don't try to change anything you are observing. Take just two minutes. Slowly open your eyes, answer: Was it easy? How many thoughts did you count? Were you able to be alert or aware of your thoughts?

4) *Observing the mind without counting, without doing anything, just observing*

   You can do this for two minutes. Were you able to observe? Were there spaces between thoughts, moments of silence or space? Was it easy?

5) *Record* all your experiences. Only when you finish can you read **attachment 22**: "Talk on Observing the Mind" by Manyu, unified consciousness teacher of Ishayas Ascension. Extract the main ideas and make a commentary based on the experience you had with the exercise.

Second strategy: Enemies of learning

There are times when our learning is blocked by limiting beliefs or judgments that have been called "enemies of learning" whose content is found in **Annex 5**.We invite you to listen to and/or read the poem "Romance de mi niña mala" (**Annex 6**) Proceed to record the following:

- Identify the enemies of the neighbor's learning of ingenuity.

- Identifies the traits of the educated being possessed by the teacher of the Girl.

- Identify which learning enemies are present in you and in what intensity (on a scale of 1 to 10).

- Formulate some actions to change the results of your behaviors in relation to these "enemies".

Select a quiet space to listen to the poem "Décima del tiempo...tiempo**".**
(**Annex 8**). Listen (hear, interpret and appreciate) without expectations, innocently.

Proceeds to:

- Record emotions and private conversations that you already know how to identify.

- Now you can use the written text on "Enemies of learning" (**Appendix 9**). Record your self-observation: which enemies of learning do you identify in each part of the poem? what would be the indicators of openness to learning? According to **Appendix 10**, do you recognize these enemies and/or indicators of openness in yourself? Remember that the importance of "noticing" is that you can "take charge of".

Third strategy: Correcting for doing rather than being

- Select a quiet space to listen to "The Song of the Cicadas" (**Appendix 18**).

- What emotions come up in you: anger, joy, anger, sadness, frustration?

- Now, you can read the text (**see appendix 3**. p. 229) Re-identify your emotions and the judgments that arise in you with each emotion. Record these emotions and the "private conversations" that accompany them.

- What actions can you take to change the results of the behaviors described in the song? We recommend reading Maturana's work: "Human formation and training", between pages 17 to 22. (**Annex 19**) You will be able to identify the impact on the child's life when *being rather than doing is corrected.*

Fourth strategy: The ways of nature

- **Learning the ways of nature:** Continue practicing breathing exercises, relaxation, visualization. Now we invite you to develop self-knowledge by identifying in yourself the elements of nature: **earth, fire, water and air. To** what extent is there a balance? You can exercise on *these through* some activities suggested in a CD (**Annex 32** - new **text** attached now) follow the instructions properly. If you can do it in a group and have someone to help you record the answers to the questions, the exercise will be much more effective.

- Now you can read **appendix 33**, entitled: *"Learning the ways of nature"*. It is convenient that this reading is not done before the exercise, in order to perform it innocently. Afterwards, you can direct it to a group of students or other people. It will help you to make distinctions to deepen your self-observation process.

The exercises you performed on the elements of nature allowed you to identify those that define you and those that are not very present in you. Become aware of this situation and incorporate more strongly the weaker ones and reduce those that are too developed. Seek balance between these elements. Become aware of when it is more convenient to show one with respect to the other. Record your experience.

Fifth strategy: Reflection for action:

Read the following thought:

> *LIFE WAS MEANT TO BE LIVED IN ETERNAL JOY,*
> *UNCONDITIONAL LOVE, ABSOLUTE FREEDOM AND UNLIMITED AWARENESS.*
> *ANYTHING LESS THAN THAT IS ABSOLUTELY DEFEATING*
> *THE PURPOSE OF BEING BORN HUMAN (MSI).*

With your life experience, what can you share as you relate it to this thought? What actions can you take to change the undesired results?

Finally, we invite you to read this story... What is the invitation contained in this story that can support integral human development?

THE LIFE YOU HOLD IS IN YOUR HANDS

A group of children knew a wise man in their
village and hatched a plan to trick him.
They would catch a live bird and go to visit the
Wise man.
One of them would hold the bird behind his
back and ask him:
<< Wise man, is the bird dead or alive?>>
If the wise man replied that he was alive, the
boy would quickly crush the bird and say:

<<No, he is dead>>.
If the wise man said: <<The bird is dead>>, the
child would show him the bird alive.
The children got the wise man to receive them.
The one holding the bird asked him:
<<Wise man, is the bird dead or alive?
The wise man remained silent for a few
moments. Then he bent down until he was at the
same height as the boy and said:
<<The life you hold is in your hands>>.

(Selection and adaptation by Beatriz Ceballos. Source: Patricia Hashuel "Conversando con un coach, No 1, October, 1999)

BC/MP/2009

Annex E

PROPOSED GENERAL PLAN FOR THE INITIAL FACE-TO-FACE SESSION

Dr. Beatriz Ceballos- Dr. Maritza Puertas

"STRATEGIES FAsESx	ACTIVITIES	Objectives-Concepts or notions	APPROXIMATE DURATION
INITIAL	Presentation in pairs You are invited to make a presentation between two people: some personal, family and professional information. Add information about aspects that are little known to others and that you would like them to know. You only give about 15 minutes. Then you voluntarily invite yourself to share your partner's presentation by pointing out everything he/she told you. Suggested questions: - Which emotion(s) can you identify as dominant in the person presented? - What indicators make you think that this or these are the dominant emotions? - What private conversations (lawsuits that were triggered and not made public) came up during the presentation? - What did you hear that he didn't tell you? - **Exploring the essence of our being** The strategy on mind observation is fully developed.	**Objective**: Self-observe the relationship between emotion, body and language or mind. Notions of basic emotions: joy, anger, sadness and fear. Notion: private conversations Notion of Effective Listening (hearing, interpreting and perceiving) Note: progressively go introducing the concepts as they appear in the sharing of the participants. If the group is very large and the time is three hours, speed up the presentations when they are very similar, staying longer with those that provide new elements.	ONE HOUR

DEVELOPMENT	**Identifying the type of observer we are being** Select one of the poems (Romance de la niña mala or Décimas del tiempo....tiempo). guidelines provided in the learning guide.	**Objective: To** identify that we are not thoughts. That we are consciousness pure. Note: if any doubt arises, invite them to flow in doubt. Little by little they will understand even if they cannot explain. The important thing is that they experience.	
	Identifying our ability to dance in life		
	Pairs are formed and will dance in silence when they hear a melody. They will connect with a marker held with the index finger of the right hand.	The enemies of learning	
	They will prevent the marker from falling off and at the same time	The trials	
	will fully enjoy the dance (they will move as freely as possible and change posture)	The language-emotion relationship	
	It is suggested to change partners after three minutes. After six minutes, stand in a circle and report on the experience: How did it feel? Was it easy? Was it comfortable and fun? What differences did you detect between the two partners?	The flow	20 minutes
	What did they realize? What did they realize?	The balance between giving and receiving	
	identify with exercise in their daily lives?	Limiting schedules	
	Note: Other questions may arise depending on the group, just keep in mind that we want to help them discover how much they flow in life, how much they are controllers, how much they are able to dance and enjoy the situations offered in life.	Body-emotion relationship	45 minutes
	Identifying nature's pathways		
	Apply the activities that appear in the learning guide related to this point.		40 minutes
	Correcting doing and not being Apply the activities of the learning guide with the song: the song of the cicadas. SLIDE PRESENTATION AND CLOSING		30 minutes

CLOSING			
			20 minutes
			20 minutes

BC/MP/ April, 2009

Annex F

WELCOME TO EXPERIENCE OUR BEING THROUGH AN
EXERCISE WE WILL CALL: Learning the ways of nature.

We invite you to experience and identify the ways of nature present in you. For this we only ask for a lot of innocence. Surrender with confidence to explore your inner self... to identify the way in which body, mind and emotion are related in you. Form a group, even if it is three people, select a large place, it can be a classroom, remove the desks so you can move freely. Wear comfortable clothes and low shoes. Each participant will stand in a circle and follow the instructions that we will begin to give in a few minutes. If there are any interruptions now, pause the recording. Once the 30 minute exercise begins you cannot stop it.

PAUSE

If you are ready, standing in a circle, pay attention to the following instructions:

Next you will hear four melodies, for each one we will ask you to move as it provokes you, contacting each of them, then we will ask you to stop and so on for each melody. It is important that you experience the exercise as it is, so that you can lead it for another group of students. Stay attentive to the instructions, without communicating with each other. Only that melody you are hearing accompanies you.

Are you ready?

- LISTEN TO THE FIRST MELODY AND BEGIN TO MOVE IN THE WAY THAT MELODY INSPIRES YOU. MINUTES OF THE MELODY Stop in this moment and close your eyes. What emotion do you experience?

What judgments accompanied that emotion?

How did your body move: heavy? light? light? light?

How do you perceive the rhythm of your breathing?

How do your muscles feel,.tense.relaxed? your posture? the position of your head?

What actions can you perform from this emotion? What actions can you not perform from this emotion?

- LISTEN TO THE SECOND MELODY AND BEGIN TO MOVE IN THE WAY THAT MELODY INSPIRES YOU .... MINUTES OF THE MELODY

Stop at this moment and close your eyes

What emotion do you experience?

What judgments accompanied that emotion?

How did your body move: heavy? light? light? light?

How do you perceive the rhythm of your breathing?

How do your muscles feel,.tense.relaxed? your posture? the position of your head?

What actions can you perform from this emotion? What actions can you not perform from this emotion?

- LISTEN TO THE THIRD MELODY AND BEGIN TO MOVE IN THE WAY THAT MELODY INSPIRES YOU. MINUTES OF THE MELODY

Stop at this moment and close your eyes

What emotion do you experience?

What judgments accompanied that emotion?

How did your body move: heavy? light? light? light?

How do you perceive the rhythm of your breathing? Slow? Soft? Accelerated?

How do your muscles feel,.tense.relaxed? your posture? the position of your head?

What actions can you perform from this emotion? What actions can you not perform from this emotion?

- KEEP YOUR EYES CLOSED AND BEGIN TO MOVE IN THE WAY THAT MELODY INSPIRES YOU. MINUTES OF THE MELODY

A FEW MINUTES LATER, WHEN THE MELODY IS FASTER, OPEN YOUR EYES AND START SCROLLING.

Annex G

GUIDELINES FOR THE CLOSING FACE-TO-FACE SESSION

Close to continue...

We are happy that you have reached this moment of culmination of the learning modules of this course of integral human development for life. No doubt your experience of stillness has developed and with it the experiential mastery that leads to spirituality. Finally, we would like to offer you some guidelines for the face-to-face session.

In this face-to-face meeting we will carry out a series of dynamics that will take you through the integrating learning axes contained in the questions of each module:

First module: "The integral formation of the Self from the development of the educated Self to the Total Self".

- How to integrate my domains (cognitive-conceptual, affective, physical, social, perceptual, moral and experiential) of the educated self towards the formation of the total self?

- How do the axes (openness, reflection and integration) of human development participate in my integral formation?

- What are my competencies as a "learner" towards the integration of the primary elements of being: body, mind, emotion and spirit?

- How do I observe, accept and re-create the essence of the human being I discover in myself?

Second module: "The development of the experiential domain of the educated being as a path to spiritual growth.

- How to quiet the mind?
- How to deepen the power of now?
- What can we do to expand our consciousness and recognize our essence?
- How to flow with the external world from inner wisdom?

What a wonderful adventure you have had...and continue to have...it doesn't stop...there is more. In the final face-to-face session you will be able to share directly the questions and reflections that have arisen throughout the course and in particular you will be able to share your experience of silence with the facilitators and your classmates. It is the process of becoming aware from the exploration of the present moment to act more consciously with your family, friends, colleagues and the community in general.

We wish you a lot of success!

We say goodbye with a story that shows the wisdom of the master... of that master that is within us. We are recognizing him as we walk the "path of the wise".

"They tell of a very rich king in India who was reputed to be indifferent to material wealth. A subject wanted to find out how he could be so rich in spite of his indifference. The king told him: "My secret will be revealed to you if you walk through my palace with a lighted candle. But if the candle goes out, I will behead you". At the end of the walk, the king asked him, "Have you discovered yet what is the source of my riches?"
The subject replied, "I couldn't see anything. I only focused on the flame not being extinguished." The king told him, "That's the secret of my riches, being very busy trying to fan my inner flame. The rest comes by itself."

Our declaration of gratitude for this opportunity to share with you, our heart vibrates with happiness, see you soon. Until every moment.

We love you. Maritza and Beatriz

BC/MP, Caracas, Caracas, November 2008

Annex H

SOME CONSIDERATIONS FOR COURSE EVALUATION

Central criterion of the evaluation:

General criterion: authenticity and openness in the answers. These will be shown in a clear, sincere and fluent way. Due to the experiential nature of the proposed learning guides, there is no good or bad answer, since there is no good or bad experience. Experience simply "is".

Specific evaluation criteria in its different modalities:

1. Each participant can show is their capacity for *openness, reflection and integration* in connection with their experiences. Select indicators derived from these definitions:

   OPENNESS: refers to the ability to adapt to oneself on a daily basis: aspirations, potentialities and limitations; open with one's community; passion for life; smiles at life. The practice of openness is linked to the ability to develop *listening* as a process where in addition to hearing, we interpret and perceive, from an empathic attitude. "The empathic way of being with another person. involves temporarily living their life, moving delicately in it without making judgments.... Being with the other in this way implies that, during that time, you set aside your own opinions and values to enter the other person's world without prejudice" (Carl Rogers).

   REFLECTION: refers to the ability to have a critical, value-oriented conscience. "Reflection is an act of detachment that releases certainty. Knowledge and certainty deny reflection because we do not reflect on what we know to be true. In the reflective gaze we operationally admit that we do not know, and we look in innocence. As a result of that gaze we can see something different and change. Reflection, as an act in language, changes our being because it changes our emotions, so that we are oriented in a different way in our relational space, outside the previous situation" (Maturana, Humberto). The ability to *question* promotes the development of this axis.

   INTEGRATION: ability to incorporate data and order them in the context of their acquisitions and experiences; coherent formation of their knowledge, skills, attitudes and values. The capacity of *synthesis* expresses the development of this axis.

2. Each participant can show levels of understanding and approach to the practice of being educated and total being. Select indicators of the traits of the educated self and the total self with the material provided in the learning guides. An approximation of the content of each trait of the educated self that can be enriched is attached.

3. Each participant can show his or her capacity to *realize* each situation or experience, rather than judging it, in order to identify in it the criteria to act in congruence with the desired objectives.

4. Exhibit performances in correspondence with the nature of the traits of the total self in the final face-to-face session.

5. Each participant may incorporate other evaluation criteria that correspond to the nature of the course.

Annex I

GUIDE TO THE SELF-EVALUATION AND CO-EVALUATION PROCESS

Dr. Beatriz Ceballos Dr.
Maritza Puertas

JUSTIFICATION

The process of self-evaluation and co-evaluation is proposed to achieve a fair appreciation of each of the participants from the "realization". We are convinced that learning as a process requires accumulated time for reflection. This means that both our successes and failures must be declared so that they become acquisitions in our training. In both cases, these are the ways of conscious learning.

In this sense, the concept of **transformational learning** is assumed, **in order to** demonstrate the levels of development of each participant's own skills in the process of self-knowledge and self-reflection.

The capacity to "realize" the successes or failures of each participant in relation to the levels (Very High, High, Medium, Low and Very Low) of self-observation and connection between theoretical postulates and lived experiences is fundamentally evaluated. Aspects correspond to a set of criteria. The indicators must be selected by the participants from the answers provided in the activities of each learning guide. One set of criteria is provided for each module. That is, guide 1 and 2 have the same criteria, guide 3 and 4 the same criteria. This is with the idea of considering the criterion of progression of all learning.

Procedure

Two support materials have been designed. One specifies the criteria to be evaluated. In addition, another summary table to be filled out by each participant once the indicators for each criterion have been defined.

Steps:

1. Answer each learning guide sequentially and progressively. It is important not to get ahead of yourself in the activities; it is the awareness of the experience in each proposed activity that

facilitates learning.

2. Formulate indicators for each criterion. In some cases we will provide you with some examples, which you can incorporate, adjust or replace with others. Annex 1

3. Proceed to assign the level of achievement (MA, A, M, B, MB) for each criterion and indicator. Appendix 2. Mark with an X your selection for self-assessment or co-assessment. Remember that the central evaluation criterion is awareness. For example, if it is assessed as very low, and relevant indicators are provided, we will assess between medium and very high. We are assessing the capacity developed in identifying what is missing. That is what we want: I might not do it well, but I will know how to do it better.

4. Analyze the result and proceed to assign an overall score for self- and co-evaluation.

Criteria

MODULE I

To show indicators that allow to appreciate the level of identification of the participant in the self-evaluation and the confrontation between theory and action.

ASPECT: Self-observation

1. Relationship between judgments, emotions and corporeality.
2. the enemies of learning
3. openness of learning
4. Praise instead of criticism

ASPECT: Connection between theory and action

5. Relationship between theoretical postulates and observed everyday situations
6. Development of each of the traits of the educated being/total being.
7. Application of each axis of development of the self: openness, reflection and integration.
8. Application of transformational learning

MODULE II

ASPECT: Self-observation

1. Correcting doing and not being
2. Relationship between judgments/emotions/body and spirit
3. Experiential domain assessment
4. Breathing practice, relaxation and visualization
5. Relevant actions towards the balance of the 4 elements of nature in the human being.
6. Identification and permanence in the space of peace, love and stillness that resides in the being.
7. Practicing the power of now
8. Practice of compassion
9. Define the most pertinent actions to achieve the desired results in the development of spirituality.

10. The death of the ego and the expansion of love

ASPECT: Connection between theory and action

1. Clear and coherent argumentation
2. Relationship between the states of consciousness and the experience of peace, love and silence obtained
3. Relationship between the state of unified consciousness and the expansion of love in the being

DISTRIBUTION OF SITES AND NUCLEI OF PARTICIPANTS IN THE ROBINSONIAN MASTER'S PROGRAM ACCORDING TO FINAL EVALUATION. PERIOD 2009- I

Name of location or No. of		FINAL EVALUATION						
Core	Registered	> 3.95	4:00 4:20	4:25 4:45	4:50- 4:70	4:75 4:95	5:00	Non-attendees
Apure	25	1	3	-	6	5	-	10
Araure	32	1	2	1	10	11	-	7
Barcelona	17	4	7	4	1	1	-	-
Caricuao	2	-	-	-	-	2	-	-
Barquisimeto	12	3	-	2	2	1	-	4
Ciudad Bolivar	6	-	1	1	4	-	-	-
Choir	12	-	-	7	4	-	-	1
Canoabo	18	1	2	3	-	1	1	10
CEPAP	3	3	-	-	-	-	-	-
El Vigia	26	-	-	5	2	13	6	-
La Grita	15	5	-	1	-	3	1	5
Los Teques	13	2	2	1	2	4	2	-
Maracay	19	2	2	2	7	2	2	2
Maturin	27	-	5	2	8	6	-	6
Postgraduate Caracas	14	3	2	1	2	1	3	2
Palo Verde	43	5	2	10	11	9	-	6
San Carlos	27	-	2	3	6	9	1	6
Santa Fe Headquarters	2	-	-	-	-	1	-	1
San Juan de los Morros	26	2	3	6	2	10	1	2
Tuy Valleys	21	4	-	1	4	6	5	1
Valera	31	2	-	3	4	9	9	4
Easter Valley	4	-	2	1	1	-	-	-
Zaraza	20	9	3	3	2	3	-	-
Idecyt	0	-	-	-	-	-	-	-
El Valle	1	1	-	-	-	-	-	-
Mucuchies	6	2	1	1		1		1
TOTAL	**422**	**50**	**39**	**58**	**78**	**98**	**31**	**68**

Annex K

DATA MATRIX OF THE PARTICIPANTS OF THE APURE, MARACAY AND SAN JUAN DE LOS MORROS NUCLEI

IDENTIF	NUCLEUS CODE	NUCLEU	SEX	CODE SEX	NOTES	RESULTS
1	1	Apure	F	1	4,50	APPROVED
2	1	Apure	M	2		NO SHOW
3	1	Apure	M	2		NO SHOW
4	1	Apure	M	2	4,00	APPROVED
5	1	Apure	M	2	4,80	APPROVED
6	1	Apure	F	1	4,55	APPROVED
7	1	Apure	F	1		NO SHOW
8	1	Apure	M	2	4,95	APPROVED
9	1	Apure	F	1	4,00	APPROVED
10	1	Apure	F	1		NO SHOW
11	1	Apure	M	2		NO SHOW
12	1	Apure	F	1	4,85	APPROVED
13	1	Apure	F	1	1,00	NOT APPROVED
14	1	Apure	M	2	4,20	APPROVED
15	1	Apure	F	1		NO SHOW
16	1	Apure	M	2		NO SHOW
17	1	Apure	M	2	4,55	APPROVED
18	1	Apure	F	1	4,65	APPROVED
19	1	Apure	F	1	4,50	APPROVED
20	1	Apure	F	1	4,85	APPROVED
21	1	Apure	F	1		NO SHOW
22	1	Apure	M	2		NO SHOW
23	1	Apure	F	1	4,50	APPROVED
24	1	Apure	F	1	4,80	APPROVED
25	1	Apure	M	2		NO SHOW
26	2	Maracay	M	2	2,00	NOT APPROVED
27	2	Maracay	F	1		NO SHOW
28	2	Maracay	M	2	1,00	NOT APPROVED
29	2	Maracay	F	1	4,00	APPROVED
30	2	Maracay	M	2	5,00	APPROVED
31	2	Maracay	M	2	4,50	APPROVED
32	2	Maracay	F	1	5,00	APPROVED
33	2	Maracay	M	2	4,75	APPROVED
34	2	Maracay	F	1	4,60	APPROVED
35	2	Maracay	F	1	4,70	APPROVED
36	2	Maracay	F	1	4,65	APPROVED
37	2	Maracay		F	1	4,70	APPROVED
38	2	Maracay		F	1	4,15	APPROVED
39	2	Maracay		M	2	4,25	APPROVED
40	2	Maracay		F	1	4,85	APPROVED
41	2	Maracay		F	1	4,50	APPROVED
42	2	Maracay		F	1	4,25	APPROVED

43	2	Maracay	F	1	4,65	APPROVED
44	2	Maracay	F	1		NO SHOW
45	3	San Juan de Los Morros	F	1	4,90	APPROVED
46	3	San Juan de Los Morros	F	1	4,90	APPROVED
47	3	San Juan de Los Morros	F	1	3,00	NOT APPROVED
48	3	San Juan de Los Morros	F	1	4,25	APPROVED
49	3	San Juan de Los Morros	F	1	4,85	APPROVED
50	3	San Juan de Los Morros	F	1	4,85	APPROVED
51	3	San Juan de Los Morros	F	1		NO SHOW
52	3	San Juan de Los Morros	F	1	4,95	APPROVED
53	3	San Juan de Los Morros	F	1	4,60	APPROVED
54	3	San Juan de Los Morros	F	1	4,80	APPROVED
55	3	San Juan de Los Morros	F	1	3,00	NOT APPROVED
56	3	San Juan de Los Morros	F	1	4,75	APPROVED
57	3	San Juan de Los Morros	F	1	4,00	APPROVED
58	3	San Juan de Los Morros	F	1	4,40	APPROVED
59	3	San Juan de Los Morros	M	2	4,25	APPROVED
60	3	San Juan de Los Morros	M	2	4,35	APPROVED
61	3	San Juan de Los Morros	F	1	4,45	APPROVED
62	3	San Juan de Los Morros	F	1	4,85	APPROVED
63	3	San Juan de Los Morros	M	2	4,15	APPROVED
64	3	San Juan de Los Morros	M	2	5,00	APPROVED
65	3	San Juan de Los Morros	M	2	4,05	APPROVED
66	3	San Juan de Los Morros	M	2		NO SHOW
67	3	San Juan de Los Morros	F	1	4,90	APPROVED
68	3	San Juan de Los Morros	F	1	4,70	APPROVED
69	3	San Juan de Los Morros	F	1	4,85	APPROVED
70	3	San Juan de Los Morros	M	2	4,25	APPROVED

CURRICULUM VITAE

My name is *MARITZA PUERTAS de RODRÍGUEZ*, born in Caracas. I obtained my degree in Education at the Central University of Venezuela (UCV), during my training as an educator I worked as a substitute teacher at the school "Consuelo Navas Tovar", once I finished my undergraduate studies I worked as an instructor at the School of Agronomy of the UCV, in Maracay, facilitating the courses of Methods and Habits of Study and Research Methodology. Later I moved to Valle de la Pascua as a teacher at the Liceo "Juan José Rondón" in Biology and as an assistant at the Instituto Universitario de Tecnología de los Llanos, holding management and teaching positions in the Office of Study Control, in the Department of Student Relations and in the chairs of Methods and Study Habits, Research Methodology and Guidance, respectively.

Postgraduate studies in Higher Education. I studied Research Methodology at the Instituto

Pedagógico Experimental de Maturín and the Ministry of Education. I won a scholarship to study in the United States, at the University of Florida (UF), where I graduated as Master of Arts in Education in the area of Scientific Research and Teaching, mention: Foundations of Education, along with the Specialization in Latin American Studies.

I served as a Librarian Assistant in the Acquisitions Department of the UF Graduate Library.

I have held administrative, teaching, research and extension positions in the Graduate Program, Research subprogram, Study Control Program, Admissions and Student Selection subprogram, Office of Planning, Budget and Institutional Evaluation and the Graduate Dean's Office of the Universidad Nacional Experimental "Simón Rodríguez" (UNESR). For five years I was Assistant Director of the Journal of Education and Human Sciences of the aforementioned Dean's Office.

I am currently a teacher-researcher in the Master's Program in Educational Sciences and a member of the Research Line "Teaching Function" (LinFunDo).

I have participated in lectures, workshops, conferences, national and international meetings and I have published as co-author in materials produced in the line, research and doctoral program at UPEL.

I have received awards from the National Commission of the System for the Recognition of Merit to Professors of National Universities. CONABA, the National Commission for the Development of Higher Education (CONADES), the Stimulus Program for Researchers (PEI) of the UNESR, the Stimulus Program for Innovation and Research (ONCTI) and recognition as a teacher at the General Hospital Dr. José Ignacio Baldó.

(*) The first 13 testimonies and the five criteria were taken from the article by Dr. Beatriz Ceballos (2009) "The experiential domain and spiritual growth in the formation of the teacher as a total being" UPEL (CIDEPD-CIGHMT).

Milton Keynes UK
Ingram Content Group UK Ltd.
UKHW040826190124
436254UK00018B/129